DK | Penguin Random House

Senior Editor Sam Atkinson
Project Art Editor Mary Sandberg
Senior Art Editor Jacqui Swan
Project Editor Sarah Carpenter
US Senior Editor Jennette ElNaggar
Illustrator Sanya Jain
Consultant Cynthia Fischer
Contributors Ann Kay, Cynthia Fischer, Sam Atkinson
Senior Picture Researcher Aditya Katyal

Managing Editor Rachel Fox
Managing Art Editor Owen Peyton Jones
Production Editors Andy Hilliard, Jacqueline Street-Elkayam
Production Controller Meskerem Berhane
UK Media Archive Romaine Werblow
Jacket Designers Akiko Kato, Juhi Sheth
Jacket DTP Designer Deepak Mittal
Senior Jackets Coordinator Priyanka Sharma-Saddi
Jacket Design Development Manager Sophia MTT

Publisher Andrew Macintyre
Art Director Karen Self
Associate Publishing Director Liz Wheeler
Publishing Director Jonathan Metcalf

First American Edition, 2024
Published in the United States by DK Publishing
1745 Broadway, 20th Floor, New York, NY 10019

Copyright © 2024 Dorling Kindersley Limited
DK, a Division of Penguin Random House LLC
24 25 26 27 28 10 9 8 7 6 5 4 3 2 1
001–336901–Mar/2024

A catalog record for this book is available from the Library of Congress.
ISBN 978-0-7440-9204-2

DK books are available at special discounts when purchased in bulk for
sales promotions, premiums, fund-raising, or educational use.
For details, contact: DK Publishing Special Markets,
1745 Broadway, 20th Floor, New York, NY 10019
SpecialSales@dk.com

Printed and bound in Hong Kong

www.dk.com

MIX
Paper | Supporting
responsible forestry
FSC™ C018179

This book was made with Forest
Stewardship Council™ certified
paper—one small step in DK's
commitment to a sustainable future.
Learn more at
www.dk.com/uk/information/sustainability

WHAT'S THE POINT OF
ART?

DK

CONTENTS

Some dates have BCE and CE after them. These are short for "before the Common Era" and "Common Era." The Common Era dates from when people think Jesus was born.

WHAT'S THE POINT OF ART?

What comes to mind when you think of art? Do you think of boring old paintings in galleries? There's much more to art than that! Humans have been creating art for thousands of years, and cultures around the world have developed their own unique artistic traditions. But the reasons for creating this art are quite similar wherever you are.

LEAVE A RECORD

Scientists believe that early humans developed language through art. They painted symbols that they could all understand. Art left behind by ancient civilizations gives us a window to the past.

KEEP THE FAITH

In religions around the world, art is used to reinforce people's beliefs. Religious art might glorify a god, or make people afraid to disobey rules.

SEND A MESSAGE

Art can be used to draw attention to a political cause through posters, banners, and graffiti in public places. Powerful images can influence or change people's minds about a particular issue.

EXPRESS YOURSELF

If you pick up a pencil and paper and draw what you feel, you're an artist! Many modern-day artists create very personal art that reflects their inner world. But artists have always put a little piece of themselves into their art.

TELL A STORY

Illustrations can really help bring a book to life and spark the imagination. But telling a story doesn't have to involve words. Even a single painting can tell a story.

DESIGN AND DECORATE

Art has a huge impact on the design of many items, such as furniture. Designers create things that make our surroundings more beautiful.

CHALLENGE TRADITION

Is a bottle of cola a piece of art? For some artists, the things we find ordinary are beautiful. They use their imagination to create new ways of seeing things.

CREATE SOMETHING BEAUTIFUL

Art can just be something that people enjoy looking at. But what counts as "beautiful" changes between cultures and over time. The idea that art must be beautiful has been challenged in modern times.

COLLABORATE AS A COMMUNITY

People come together in public places to create pieces of art, such as murals, that encourage a sense of community. Artists may work with groups of people to clean up a neglected part of a town or city.

SHOW YOUR STATUS

Just as today we want to look our best in a photo, people once had portraits painted wearing their finest clothes and surrounded by things that showed off their wealth or power.

WHAT'S THE POINT OF LOOKING AT
ANCIENT ART?

Art has always been an important part of life—even the earliest humans struggling for survival made time to create art. Cave paintings and other prehistoric artworks offer us an insight into the lives and thoughts of people who lived many thousands of years ago, before the invention of writing. As time moved on, ancient civilizations such as the Egyptians, Greeks, and Romans created many great works of art that tell us much about their cultures. They were also great artisans—Greek techniques for crafting lifelike sculptures haven't really been improved upon in the last 2,500 years.

HOW TO BE UNDERSTOOD

No one knows for certain why early humans made cave art, but due to the sheer amount of it, we know that art was important to them. Some scientists believe that cave art was how humans started expressing themselves. The very act of making a mark on walls prompted a new way of thinking that led to the development of human language.

Claw marks left behind by animals inspired the first cave art.

1 The earliest pieces of cave art that have *been* found are scratches on walls, similar to those made by animals, such as bears and lions. The Neanderthal people, an extinct relative of modern humans, made these scratches around 75,000 years ago.

2 Early modern humans discovered they could crush rocks to powder to make paint. Charcoal provided the color black, and other minerals added yellow and brown. Artists would have had to prepare their tools and paints *before* entering the caves, which were often dark inside.

3 Cave art developed over thousands of years until humans created an early stenciling technique. They placed their hands on walls and blew paint over them to make overlapping prints.

Paint was mixed with saliva and "sprayed" out.

4 In the light of the burning flames, humans would depict stags, bison, and horses—animals that they hunted. Some scientists believe that they were developing symbols to use as a way of communicating with each other.

Drawings of animals may have been symbolic, much like words.

DID YOU KNOW?

First storytellers
Cave art in the Lascaux Cave in France is currently estimated to be around 17,000 years old. Scientists believe that some drawings in the cave tell stories. Images of animals overlap to represent movement, like in a cartoon.

Cave painting, possibly showing a bear walking, at the Lascaux Cave

VENUS FIGURINES

Sculptures of female forms made in prehistoric Europe are often known as Venus figurines, after the Roman goddess of love. Made from mammoth ivory, the *Venus of Brassempouy* is possibly the world's oldest realistic depiction of a human face.

Venus of Brassempouy, c.25,000 years ago

Newspaper Rock in Utah is covered in petroglyphs (images scratched into a surface), some of which date from around 2,000 years ago.

The ivory *Löwenmensch* ("lion-person") figurine, found in a cave in Germany, is the oldest-known statue ever discovered, at around 41,000 years old.

The Olmec culture (1200–400 BCE) of southern Mexico sculpted giant stone heads from basalt boulders.

This terracotta figure of a bird-man dates from Nigeria's Nok culture (500 BCE–200 CE).

The Raimondi Stone of the Chavin culture (1000–200 BCE) shows a figure known as the Staff God.

EARLY ART AROUND THE WORLD

The first art didn't spring up in a single place and spread around the world. As people settled down and civilizations developed in different regions, different artistic traditions emerged. Artworks created by carving into or sculpting stone, wood, clay, metal, bones, or ivory were often the earliest examples of these traditions.

DID YOU KNOW?

Mask of Agamemnon, gold funeral mask from Mycenae, Greece, c.1550–1500 BCE

Ancient gold
Gold was a rare precious metal that could be found in certain rivers during ancient times. It was often used to create art and jewelry for royalty as it was expensive but easy to shape.

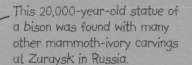

This 20,000-year-old statue of a bison was found with many other mammoth-ivory carvings at Zuraysk in Russia.

CHINESE BRONZE

During the Chinese Bronze Age (2000–256 BCE), making offerings of food and drink to the dead was a common practice. Noble and wealthy families had beautiful and ornate vessels crafted by artisans to hold the offerings to their ancestors.

Bronze vessel from the Shang or early Zhou period (c.1600–771 BCE)

The Royal Tombs of Ur in southern Iraq held a pair of matching gold and lapis luzuli statues, known as the *Ram in a Thicket*, dating to about 2600–2400 BCE.

The pottery of the Majiayao culture (3200–2650 BCE) along China's Huang River is known for its curved line decoration.

A *Dogū* ("earthen figure" in Japanese) is a small figurine of the Jomon period (14,000–400 BCE).

This miniature ceramic ox-drawn cart was a children's toy of the Indus Valley civilization (c.3300–1300 BCE).

The *Ambum Stone* (c.1500 BCE) of New Guinea is carved in the shape of some kind of animal— its original purpose is unknown.

FIRST AUSTRALIAN ROCK ART

There is a continuous tradition of First Australian art that has lasted for more than 20,000 years and is still alive today. Some ancient rock-art sites are still being added to by First Australian artists to this day.

Aboriginal rock art at Nourlangie, Kakadu National Park, Northern Territory, Australia

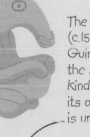

13

HOW TO SET THINGS IN STONE

Ancient Mesopotamia was a region in what is now the Middle East. The world's first cities sprang up here around the 4th millennium BCE. Much of the art that has survived from this time is in the form of stone sculptures and reliefs (raised carvings on a surface). Though stone was a scarce resource in the area, it was used to create art for various purposes—for decoration, religious reasons, and to show power and authority.

DID YOU KNOW?

The Standard of Ur
Discovered in the 1920s, the Standard of Ur is a wooden rectangular object decorated with lapis lazuli (a bright blue stone) and shells. One side depicts a battle, while the other shows the spoils of war.

The Standard of Ur, c.2600–2400 BCE

STATUES OF POWER

The Sumerian ruler Gudea of Lagash commissioned several statues of himself from diorite—an extremely hard stone that had to be imported—to ensure that his memorials would survive. These statues were not portraits but symbols of power to be placed in temples.

CYLINDER SEALS

Stone cylinder seals were engraved with patterns and images of gods, humans, and animals. These designs were unique to the seal's owner. When rolled across wet clay, they left an impression of the design, and they were used to mark property or make legal agreements

As the clay dried, the image hardened into a long-lasting impression.

The Hittites represented the sphinx as a lion with a female human head.

GATEWAY GUARDIANS

By 1350 BCE, the Hittite Empire, centered in modern-day Türkiye, had grown to encompass parts of northern Mesopotamia. At entrances to their cities, the Hittites carved monumental sculptures of lions, warriors, and mythical creatures such as the sphinx. These gateway guardian figures were common in ancient cultures of the eastern Mediterranean Sea.

ROYAL RELIEFS

The Assyrians of northern Mesopotamia frequently carved scenes of lion hunts into the walls of palaces. For the Assyrians, lion hunting was more than a royal sport—it also had religious implications. Images of rulers ridding the land of lions showed their role as champions of the gods, cleansing the land of evil.

BRICK ART

The Babylonians came to power in the 2nd millennium BCE. Their most well-known artworks are their animal reliefs, produced on glazed, colored bricks. The creatures were first modeled in damp clay, which was then cut up into bricks. The most impressive examples were on the Ishtar Gate, the spectacular entrance to the capital city of Babylon.

HOW TO BE IMMORTAL

In some ancient cultures, people had such a strong belief in a life after death that they wanted to take their possessions into the next life. When a high-ranking person died, they were often buried with their belongings. These might be artworks specifically created for the dead to take with them, some of which were meant to ease their journey to the land of the dead. Huge amounts of time, money, and skill went into producing this art.

DID YOU KNOW?

Tutankhamun
In 1922, archaeologists rediscovered the tomb of Tutankhamun, who came to the throne in 1333 BCE. The tomb contained thousands of precious artifacts, including the golden death mask that protected the pharaoh's mummified head.

Mask of Tutankhamun

In the tomb of Tutankhamun, wonderful objects were piled on top of each other for the pharaoh to take with him.

Pharaohs were buried with chariots so they could lead an army in the afterlife.

ANCIENT EGYPTIAN TOMB

Much of Egyptian life was dedicated to what happens when you die. The rulers of ancient Egypt, the pharaohs, were buried in elaborate tombs. Whole rooms near the central burial chamber were piled high with precious treasures and useful items.

The soldiers all have different headgear, hairstyles, and facial expressions.

TERRACOTTA ARMY

Chinese emperor Qin Shi Huangdi was buried in 210 BCE in a vast tomb that contained an "army" of more than 7,000 life-size terracotta warriors. Construction of the army began in 246 BCE and took nearly 40 years. The warriors were buried with the emperor to protect him in the afterlife.

Terracotta chariot

The army was originally painted in bright colors, but these faded quickly after the figures were dug up.

SHIP BURIAL

In 1939 at Sutton Hoo, England, archaeologists discovered a huge wooden longship with a burial chamber full of treasures, including items made from gold and silver. The grave probably belonged to a 7th-century Anglo-Saxon king.

Sutton Hoo helmet

Military equipment laid near the body suggests the dead person was a strong leader.

EGYPTIAN TOMB PAINTING

Most of the art that survives from ancient Egypt has to do with death and the afterlife. One of the main concerns of Egyptian life was ensuring happiness even in death, so tomb painters even provided instructions in images to help the gods care properly for the dead. These instructions were painted onto tomb walls, particularly for important people such as the pharaohs.

DID YOU KNOW?

Spells for the afterlife

A wealthy and powerful person was often buried with a scroll version of the *Book of the Dead*. It contained spells that were believed to help the person find their way to the afterlife.

The *Book of the Dead*

1 On a smooth, plastered wall, tomb painters applied a grid using a string dipped in red pigment. They outlined the figures according to the grid, to make sure the size and proportions were correct.

The walls were smoothed and prepared for painting with a flat plastering tool.

2 Close to the large paintings were stories of the dead people in the tombs. These stories were written in hieroglyphs—small pictures and symbols that together made up the ancient Egyptian system of writing.

3 Once the outline was complete, the artist filled in the color. Human figures were drawn with the head and limbs shown from the side (in profile) and the torso facing forward. This allowed the artist to show as much detail as possible.

PIGMENTS

Ancient Egyptians made paints by digging up minerals (such as those shown below) and grinding them into a powder Known as a pigment. This powder was mixed with a binder, such as gum arabic (a gluelike substance from certain trees), to help it stick when applied to a surface.

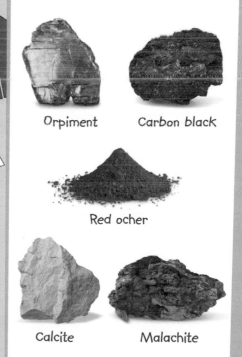

Orpiment

Carbon black

Red ocher

Calcite

Malachite

Minerals were crushed into powder with a pigment grinder.

HOW TO CRAFT PERFECTION

Exciting new ideas flourished in ancient Greece around 500 BCE. At this time, great thinkers searched for the most perfect—or ideal—theories about all kinds of subjects, from science and politics to art and drama. In art, Greek artists wanted to create sculptures that expressed the "ideal" human figure. This has been an enormously influential idea in Western art ever since.

Many ancient Greek buildings and sculptures are totally white today, but they were once painted in bright colors.

BALANCED BUILDINGS

The ancient Greeks admired balance and harmony in many areas of life. This drive to create perfection can be seen in their architecture, through symmetrical buildings that are clearly organized in their designs.

DID YOU KNOW?

Bronze statues
Many ancient Greek bronze statues were lost or melted down for their valuable metal. A lot of the "Greek" statues we see today are actually marble or bronze copies of Greek originals, or copy the Greek style.

One of the Riace bronzes, probably Greek and from the 5th century BCE

THE HUMAN IDEAL

The ancient Greek interest in science led artists to show poses and muscles in a more lifelike way than ever before. However, at the same time, these ideal human bodies did not reflect reality.

The head usually turns to one side in contrapposto poses.

Greek sculptor Polyclitus appears to have worked with proportions that divide the body into seven parts, based on the size of the head.

PERFECT PROPORTION

A love of math made the Greeks fascinated by proportion. They seem to have had set ideas about how the size of one part of the body relates to the whole. They used these ideas to create perfect, beautiful sculptures.

One hip is higher than the other to create a relaxed pose.

ART CONNECTIONS

Form and function
Ancient Greek pots also show perfectionism. For example, the shape and decoration of water jars were lovely and balanced, but they also had the perfect form: two side handles for carrying and a back handle for pouring.

Greek water jar, c.510 BCE

One knee is usually bent for a more natural stance.

CONTRAPPOSTO

Developed by ancient Greek sculptors, the contrapposto pose makes statues look more natural and relaxed. In a typical contrapposto pose, one straight leg takes the body's weight, and other body parts tilt away from each other (contrapposto means "counterbalance" or "set against" in Italian).

HOW TO DECORATE YOUR ROOM

The ancient Romans decorated their homes to cover the bare walls. From around 200 BCE, artists covered interiors with frescoes—paintings applied directly onto wet plaster as it dried on the wall, so they became part of the wall itself. Over time, the Romans developed different styles of fresco, to create the illusion of lush greenery or architectural details.

1 The rooms in the homes of the early ancient Romans were often quite small and claustrophobic, and some didn't even have windows. Those who could afford it began to employ artists to paint the bare walls to make the rooms feel brighter and more spacious.

Layers of stucco, a type of plaster, were applied to make parts of the wall appear raised.

DID YOU KNOW?

Buried in ash
Mount Vesuvius on the coast of southern Italy erupted in 79 CE, covering several towns with lava. This hardened into rock, preserving many of the paintings in the buildings that lay buried. Excavations have taught us much of what we know about Roman painting today.

Villa of Publius Fannius Synistor, Boscoreale, c.40 BCE

2 At first, the Romans painted the walls to look like they were constructed from more expensive materials. Artists applied paints of various colors in the shape of blocks to create the illusion of a patchwork of marble slabs. This is often called the masonry style because the walls appeared to be made of stone.

4 From 20 BCE, painters stopped depicting large scenes, and frescoes became more decorative. Walls were painted in single solid colors, and divided up by architectural details that framed beautiful miniature illustrations. The result was a bit like an art gallery.

Mosaics
Wealthy Romans typically covered their floors with mosaics—tiny tiles of colored stone or glass made into patterns or images. Unlike frescoes, many survive today, giving us a vivid picture of Roman life.

Mosaic detail, 2nd century BCE

Realistic depictions helped create the illusion that rooms looked on to the outside world.

3 Later fresco painters developed the idea of illusion further. They created imaginary landscapes full of buildings or trees and fields. These paintings could make you feel like you were in a busy city or a beautiful garden.

5 The final style of Roman wall painting, from around 20 CE, was a mix-up of all the earlier styles. Artists gave free rein to their imaginations, creating busy, colorful—and sometimes chaotic—spaces with lots to look at.

WHAT'S THE POINT OF LOOKING AT
MEDIEVAL AND RENAISSANCE ART?

In medieval Europe and the Middle East, most art was produced for use in Christian and Muslim places of worship. At this time, artists around the world—with some exceptions, such as those in imperial China—were generally seen as skilled craftspeople. In Europe, that all changed during a period known as the Renaissance, when some artists, particularly in Italy, became international superstars. The artists of the Renaissance wanted to make their art look as perfectly realistic as the world around them, and were celebrated as creative geniuses.

HOW TO WORSHIP AN ICON

In Christianity, icons—depictions of supernatural beings or saintly humans—are used to bring worshippers closer to the object of their faith. Many other religions create art that makes a connection between the human realm and the divine. In some religions, depictions of divine beings are seen as stand-ins for the beings themselves, while in others they are focuses for ritual and meditation.

Hindu gods are depicted with multiple limbs, each of which represents a different aspect of the god.

HINDU PROCESSION

The art that depicts the many gods of Hinduism is designed to enable *darshan*, a personal connection with the divine that is concentrated through the god's image. Processions in which statues of gods are carried down the street allow everyone to connect with the divine through *darshan*.

Detail of mosaic in Hagia Sophia,
Istanbul, Türkiye, 13th century

Great Buddha Dordenma,
Bhutan, 2015

Tile showing a modern Navajo
sand painting

CHRISTIAN ART

From the 4th century CE, icons of
Biblical figures and saints were
created for Christian worship.
The figures always faced
outward, allowing the worshipper
to connect with Christ and
the saints.

Representations of
the gods carry their
attributes objects
that are associated
with them.

BUDDHIST ART

Statues of the Buddha serve as
a reminder to worshippers of the
Buddha's virtues in life, but they
are also used as a focus during
meditation. The Buddha is shown
in one of three asanas (poses):
standing, seated, or reclining.

NAVAJO ART

Sand paintings are used in Navajo
rituals. A Navajo word for the
paintings means "places where the
gods come and go" as the art is
created to ask the gods for aid in
healing or for good harvests.

DID YOU KNOW?

Shinto guardians

Inari is the *kami* (god or spirit)
of foxes, rice, and good fortune
in Shinto, a Japanese religion.
Almost all shrines dedicated to
Inari in Japan are guarded by a
pair of *kitsune* (fox) statues, one
male and one female. These
messengers of Inari are also
considered to be Inari itself.

Kitsune statue, Fushimi
Inari Shrine, Kyoto, Japan

HOW TO STICK TO A PATTERN

In the art of Islam, a religion that began in the 7th century CE, pictures of people and animals have often been frowned upon, and at various times even forbidden. This is because making likenesses of the world was seen as too close to God's role as the ultimate creator. In place of figurative art, a tradition of patternmaking has always been essential to Islamic art.

GEOMETRIC PATTERNS

Much Islamic art is devoted to interlocking geometric patterns. These beautiful designs are mathematically precise and could potentially repeat forever. Artists can use these designs to represent the perfect and infinite nature of God.

ART CONNECTIONS

Islamic miniatures

Art from the Islamic world that deals with secular (nonreligious) topics can be figurative. Miniature paintings that illustrate books show complex scenes with precise details of people and animals.

Mughal miniature from the *Akbarnama* of Abul Fazl, c.1590

Floral arabesque at Jamali Kamali Mosque, Delhi, India

ARABESQUE DESIGNS

In contrast to sharp-edged geometric designs, the style of Islamic pattern known as arabesque is filled with flowing, repeating patterns and motifs (decorative designs) based on nature. The sweep of a vine or the curve of flower petals can inspire entire walls of tilework.

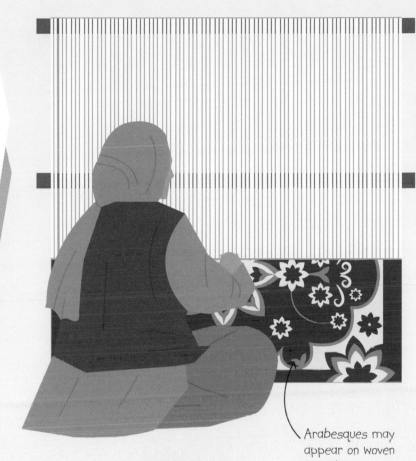

Arabesques may appear on woven carpets.

TRY IT OUT
TESSELLATING PATTERNS

When shapes in a pattern fit together with no gaps or overlaps, it is called a tessellating pattern. You can make your own using different colors of paper. Start by cutting out an even number of squares and triangles of similar sizes. Then fit the pieces together in repeating patterns, gluing them onto a larger sheet of paper to hold them in place.

Experiment to see how many repeating patterns you can make out of the same shapes.

HOW TO WRITE BEAUTIFULLY

In some cultures, calligraphy (decorative handwriting) is seen as one of the greatest forms of art. In imperial China, an artist's choice of brushstroke could express their personality and communicate more than the text itself to the reader. In medieval Christian and Islamic cultures, religious texts were considered worthy of the time and attention to make them *beautiful* because they revealed the will of God.

When writing Chinese calligraphy, the brush is held vertically.

Medieval scribes copied texts at purpose-built desks in rooms called scriptoriums.

CHRISTIAN MANUSCRIPTS

In Europe, from the 6th century onward, books were handmade by monks and nuns for large churches or important people. Scribes would copy the words, and artists would decorate manuscripts to beautify the word of God.

CHINESE CALLIGRAPHY

Since the 3rd century CE, calligraphy has been a major art form in China. A Chinese scholar was expected to master both painting and calligraphy. The two forms of art often appeared in the same artworks.

ART CONNECTIONS

Calligraphy in architecture

In the religion of Islam, images are not allowed in religious buildings. For centuries, Islamic artists have used calligraphy of verses from the Koran to decorate their walls.

Calligraphy carved into the Taj Mahal tomb in India

A qalam is a type of reed pen used for Islamic calligraphy.

ISLAMIC CALLIGRAPHY

Early Islamic thought considered depictions of the world to be offensive to God, so calligraphy developed in the 7th century as a form of artistic expression. Books, pottery, and metalware were all decorated with beautiful Arabic script.

HOW TO RECORD THE TIMES

Art can be a way to preserve history, without the need for words. However, when monarchs and government officials commission these types of works from artists, they often have a strong point of view they would like to be presented. So it is their particular version of events that is handed down through the ages. Nevertheless, art can record important moments in history and give us information about civilizations and their ways of life.

Ivory tusks, wooden staffs, brass bells, and bronze heads were placed on royal altars.

DID YOU KNOW?

Stolen treasures
The Benin Kingdom's people, the Edo, made many kinds of art. In 1897, British soldiers stormed the oba's palace and stole all their treasures. Debates continue today about whether the art should remain in London's British Museum or be returned to Nigeria.

Benin Bronze plaque

BENIN BRONZES

Bronze sculptures from the West African Kingdom of Benin (modern-day Nigeria) recorded details of social history and honored important ancestors. They often presided over altars belonging to Benin obas (rulers) and their families.

Head of an oba

A portion of the Bayeaux Tapestry

BAYEAUX TAPESTRY

At 230 feet (70 meters) long, the Bayeaux Tapestry tells a detailed story through embroidery on cloth. The Norman Conquest of England in 1066 is portrayed in scenes designed to emphasize the victory and power of William the Conqueror.

ART CONNECTIONS

Modern murals

In the Mexican National Palace, three large walls are covered with important scenes from Mexico's history painted by 20th-century muralist Diego Rivera. His work was inspired by the wall art of Indigenous Mexican peoples.

Mexico Today and Tomorrow
(the South Wall), 1935, Diego Rivera

MAYAN MURALS

The 8th-century Mayan murals (wall paintings) at Bonampak, Mexico, are some of the finest surviving examples of Mayan painting. Colorful imagery portrays many aspects of life, such as battles and celebrations.

Mayan mural at Bonampak

33

HOW TO BE DEVOUT

From the late 14th to early 15th century, a new style of art developed in Europe's royal households (courts) called International Gothic. The wealthy patrons of art in this style were often concerned with showing how devout (deeply religious) they were. They paid for expensive religious paintings and illustrated books, even asking artists to include them in biblical scenes.

Book of hours, 1430–1435, workshop of Bedford Master

The King who ordered this work appears in the painting.

PICTURING PATRONS

Most paintings were religious, but the wealthy nobles and monarchs who ordered works from artists wanted images that reflected luxurious court life. Patrons liked to appear in paintings they paid for to show that they were cultured, rich, and devout.

Images featured elegant clothes and delicate, detailed decoration.

RICH COLORS

Gold decoration and strong colors looked luxurious. An expensive pigment made from the semiprecious stone lapis lazuli was used for bright blues and stars were often in gold leaf.

Landscapes had realistic details, and often featured grand buildings.

Tapestries

Hanging large tapestries on the walls of castles made rooms warmer and provided areas for images. Intricately woven, richly colored works in the International Gothic style showed popular courtly interests such as hunting.

Detail of *Boar and Bear Hunt* from the Devonshire Hunting Tapestries, 1425–1430, probably made in Arras, France

Graceful folds of fabric create elegantly curving lines.

LIFELIKE FACES

At this time, artists were becoming more interested in showing reality, so faces are often more lifelike than in the past. There were increasing numbers of wealthy merchants who bought art and they wanted aspects of it to reflect their own world.

HOW TO PAINT WITH INK AND BRUSH

Painting with ink has been an art in China for thousands of years. From as early as the Tang Dynasty (618–907), Chinese scholars were expected to master the art, which took years to perfect. To create work of high quality required great skill and precision, and each painting could include a variety of styles, depending on how the artist applied the ink with the brush.

In a "boned" style of Chinese painting, there are outlines that may be filled in with washes.

SHAN SHUI

Ink paintings of landscapes, known as *shan shui* ("mountain-water") in Chinese, have been popular since the late Tang Dynasty. Artists have been less concerned with realism than with capturing the idea of nature as a peaceful place to withdraw from the routines of daily life.

CALLIGRAPHY

Painting and calligraphy—decorative handwriting—were often combined in the same work, as both arts were highly regarded. They also required the same tools—ink, brushes, and an absorbent surface, such as rice paper or silk.

In a "boneless" style of Chinese painting, brush marks create shapes without visible outlines.

BRUSHSTROKES

The skillful application of pressure by the artist allows the same brush to produce different types of strokes, from the broad, heavy strokes of bamboo stalks to the quick, light strokes that represent leaves.

Chinese pottery

The earliest civilizations of China produced pottery, and this craft has held an important place in Chinese art ever since. Figurines, particularly of horses, were popular in the Tang Dynasty, and Chinese porcelain is known around the world.

Tang Dynasty ceramic horse

SEALS

The artist might use seals (identifying marks applied with a stamp) to sign their name on a painting. Artists often used two seals for their name—each representing ying or yang, opposing but balanced energies in Chinese philosophy.

Red paste is applied to a stamp then pressed onto the paper or silk.

Stamp

CREATING INK

Traditional Chinese ink comes in a solid stick form. This inkstick is ground against an inkstone, and the resulting powder is mixed with water on the inkstone to create a liquid ink.

Bristles on a painting brush are made from animal hair, closely packed together to hold a good amount of ink.

Inkstone

Bamboo handle

Inkstick

TRY IT OUT
LIMITING YOUR PALETTE

Create a painting using only shades of a single color. Use darker shades for things in the foreground (at the front of the painting) and lighter shades for the background. How does the effect this creates compare to using many colors?

HOW TO HAVE FRESH IDEAS

Exciting new ideas about the world and art spread far and wide between the 14th and 16th centuries. One reason for this was that different peoples were brought together by expanding worldwide trade routes as well as wars, so they influenced each other. At the same time, there was a huge interest in looking afresh at ideas from ancient times. This momentous explosion of fresh ideas and art is called the Renaissance, French for "rebirth."

FLORENCE

Key cities grew and became flourishing centers of trade and art, especially in Italy, which was a major center of the Renaissance. As the city of Florence needed art for grand churches, palaces, and public buildings, artists flocked to work there.

Prominent people such as Lorenzo de' Medici, from a great Italian family of bankers and merchants, were patrons of the arts.

PATRONS

Flourishing trade connections made rulers and growing numbers of European merchants and bankers rich and powerful. These patrons commissioned (ordered) grand art and architecture to show their wealth and importance.

Artist
MICHELANGELO

Italian sculptor and painter Michelangelo was viewed as a master in his lifetime, and still is today. Considering himself primarily a sculptor, he reluctantly began painting the Sistine Chapel ceiling in 1508. Michelangelo showed great skill and endurance in finishing the ceiling.

Ceiling of Sistine Chapel, Vatican, Rome, 1508–1512

38

Pope Julius II summoned Michelangelo to Rome, Italy, to paint the ceiling of the Sistine Chapel.

CELEBRITIES

Rich people competed with each other to commission the finest artists, and those in greatest demand, such as Michelangelo, became celebrities. The status of artists started rising in the Renaissance, and they were admired as individuals with special talents.

Studying the ancient Greek philosophers Plato (left) and Aristotle (right) opened up new theories about the world around us.

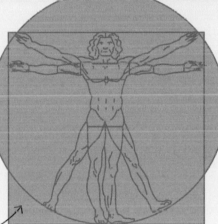

Humanism brought together science, religion, and philosophy and promoted ideas such as ideal proportions for the human body.

CLASSICS

Renaissance artists had a new kind of appreciation for ancient Greek and Roman texts, sculptures, and buildings. This was because Renaissance art moved toward greater realism, and much ancient sculpture, although idealized, had realistic-looking aspects.

HUMANISM

Art's greater realism at this time is linked with humanism— a Renaissance way of thinking that gave importance to the potential of human beings within a religious framework. It was influenced by the philosophies of ancient Greece and Rome and of the Islamic world.

A RENAISSANCE ARTIST'S WORKSHOP

During the Renaissance, the status of artists rose, and those who were in demand had to produce lots of pieces. But they didn't have to do all the work on their own. Master artists ran big, busy workshops, where apprentice artists trained and helped the master with their tasks.

Junior apprentices did simple tasks, such as sweeping up.

Master artist

Wealthy patron

PREPARING MATERIALS

Apprentices usually began their training around 11 years old, and it might last several years. Almost all apprentices were boys. Their first art tasks included grinding paint pigments and preparing surfaces for painting.

Preparing paints from pigment

Painting "gesso" (a chalky, sticky substance) on a canvas to prepare it for painting

COMMISSIONS

Artists relied on their patrons to commission (order) works from them. Once the patron had discussed the commission and made their requirements clear, the master artist would decide how the workshop staff would produce the work.

Young apprentices

Workshops were often filled with sculptures being made or copied.

DRAWING

After basic tasks, apprentices learned to draw. First they copied artists' drawings. Then they drew three-dimensional objects. This prepared them for the next stage—drawing live models, which were frequently their fellow apprentices.

More advanced apprentice

Plaster cast (copy) of a sculpture

Apprentice painting in a basic outline

Some artists trained to sculpt, as well as paint.

PAINTING

From drawing, apprentices moved on to painting. They might paint less important areas of their master's works, such as outlines or landscape backgrounds, or maybe a whole picture—pupils were trained to copy their master's style.

HOW TO GET SOME PERSPECTIVE

One new idea that completely changed art during the period Known as the Renaissance was the development of linear perspective in the early 15th century. Perspective is a method of creating a realistic sense of depth on a flat surface. Italian Architect Filippo Brunelleschi is said to have demonstrated his technique of linear perspective in his accurate painting of the Florence Baptistery.

1 Some form of perspective technique was Known to ancient Greek and Roman artists, but in medieval Europe, a sense of depth was less important in art. Figures in medieval paintings may have been sized depending on their importance in the scene, rather than to give an accurate depiction of the world.

The buildings look too small for the monks.

The tree seems smaller than the people.

The Ecstasy of St. Francis, 1297–1299, fresco attributed to Giotto di Bondone

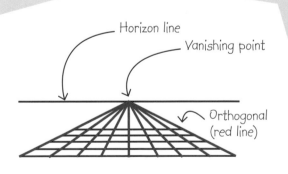

Horizon line

Vanishing point

Orthogonal (red line)

2 To create more realism, Brunelleschi pioneered a system that was based on drawing various lines. The horizon line divided the sky and the ground. Orthogonals (diagonal lines) started in the foreground, but all met up on the horizon line at a place called the vanishing point.

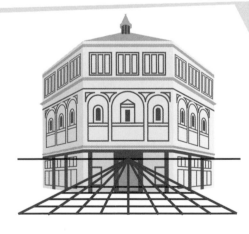

3 Brunelleschi may have used the linear perspective that this grid created to help him plan out his recreation of the Florence Baptistery, so that it had a realistic sense of depth on a flat surface.

4 It is said that after creating his painting, Brunelleschi checked its accuracy as follows. He made an eyehole at the vanishing point he had used to paint the building, then looked at the painting in a mirror. He held this up against the actual Baptistery so that he could move the mirror around and check the angles and lines he had drawn.

The eyehole in the painting allowed Brunelleschi to look through it from the back.

Brunelleschi held the painting and mirror so that the eyehole lined up with the same point on the building.

Brunelleschi held the painting facing away from him so he could see it in the mirror.

The mirror reflected the image of the painting so that Brunelleschi could check the angles against the real building.

By moving the mirror out of his line of sight and back again, Brunelleschi was able to compare the lines on his painting with the original.

TRY IT OUT
FORESHORTENING

Another technique that Renaissance artists used to create a sense of depth in their paintings is known as foreshortening. It uses the fact that things look distorted when viewed at certain distances or angles. You can see this yourself by standing in front of a mirror. If you hold your hand up to your face, your arm will look a normal size in proportion to the rest of you. As you move your hand toward the mirror, not only will it appear larger but your arm will also appear to get shorter as it extends.

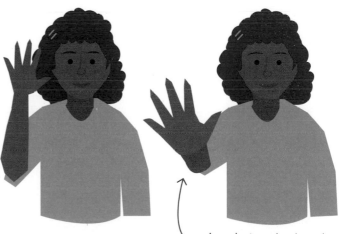

Arm is foreshortened

HOW TO DO YOUR RESEARCH

The Renaissance period was filled with stimulating new theories and a curiosity about our world. As part of this, artists such as Leonardo da Vinci became interested in approaches that would improve the realism of art. They used preparatory drawings (sketches) more and more, to play with ideas and research aspects of their work—from studying the body to finding the best composition (arrangement).

TESTING OUT IDEAS

Experimenting was the key to unlocking creativity. As the first step toward creating a painting, many artists made sketches of various ideas or rough versions of a composition, often in pen and ink.

Paper became more available in the Renaissance, which encouraged sketching.

Da Vinci even dissected dead people to learn more about anatomy.

STUDYING THE NATURAL WORLD

In their quest to capture realistic-looking detail in their work, artists studied human bodies, plants, and animals closely and made repeated drawings. These drawings could then be referred to or copied when making a final painting.

Some models would have been art workshop assistants.

WORKING OUT COMPOSITIONS

Artists drew real people posing in front of them (life drawing) to perfect the poses of people shown in their paintings. They then incorporated these studies into sketches of complete compositions.

Artist
LEONARDO DA VINCI

Italian artist da Vinci's research spanned a huge range of both scientific and artistic knowledge. His famous *Mona Lisa* portrait shows a great understanding of the face's anatomical structure and also cleverly uses *sfumato* (soft shading) to create harmony.

Many of da Vinci's drawings were just for background research, to give him greater understanding.

USING THE RESEARCH

Armed with sketches of whole compositions, studies of details, and drawings of figures in different poses, artists could produce more advanced drawings that showed how a finished painting would look.

Mona Lisa, c.1503–1519

HOW TO MAKE ART TRUE TO LIFE

While Renaissance artists in Italy created grand images based on classical ideals, northern European artists of the 15th and 16th centuries were more interested in recording things as they really were. Artists made skillful, super lifelike art filled with lots of detail, helped by advances in oil painting and printing techniques. Their art was also packed with symbols that would have been widely understood at the time.

An entire miniature version of the scene from behind is shown in great detail in the mirror.

Thin, built-up glazes (layers) of oil paint produce lifelike skin tones.

Light and shade create depth to portray crisp fabric folds.

The dog may symbolize loyalty. The texture of the fur is captured exactly.

The Arnolfini Portrait, 1434, Jan van Eyck

OIL PAINTING

The use of oil paint was developed by northern artists, helping them to create incredibly lifelike images. Oils dry slowly, so changes can be made, and they work well when used thickly, thinly, or for tiny details.

Globe showing the stars

Skull

Sundial

Lute (with a broken string)

Hymn book

The Ambassadors, 1533, Hans Holbein the Younger

SYMBOLISM

Realistic styles made symbols (where an object or person represents an idea) extra powerful. In German artist Holbein's *The Ambassadors*, objects' exact meanings are unknown, but a major theme is probably the fleeting nature of life on Earth.

Woodcuts were made by cutting an image into wood, inking it, and pressing it onto paper.

PRINTMAKING

German artists excelled at creating finely detailed prints, made by cutting images into wood (woodcuts) or metal (engravings). Newly developed German printing presses helped spread these images to a wider audience.

The Annunciation, c.1475–1482, Martin Schongauer

Artist ALBRECHT DÜRER

German artist Dürer is seen as a leading light of the Northern Renaissance. He painted many self portraits and religious scenes, but his reputation also rests on his incredible prints. They are filled with delicate lines that create precise, realistic images with subtle light and shade. Dürer's human figures are shown in a range of lifelike shapes and sizes, rather than one ideal form.

A Knight, Death, and the Devil, 1513

47

Nazca Lines

The Nazca people of southern Peru (100 BCE–650 CE) cut shapes into the desert by removing gravel to reveal lighter earth underneath. The lines can be seen only from the air, and their purpose is unknown.

Nazca Lines in the shape of a monkey with a spiral tail

TEOTIHUACÁN

From around 200 CE, the skyline of Teotihuacán, the most powerful city in the Mexican region, was dominated by the Temple of the Sun. Rising to a height of 230 feet (70 meters), the exterior of the building was covered in painted plaster, shaped into mythological scenes.

Al apaec

MOCHE

Based around the city of Moche near modern-day Trujillo in north coastal Peru, the Moche people built huge temples. Designs inside the Temple of the Moon illustrated the head of a bloodthirsty god, Al apaec.

HOW TO BUILD A MONUMENT

Much of the art of ancient Indigenous cultures of South America and Mesoamerica (a name for Mexico and Central America) did not survive the arrival of European invaders in the 16th century. However, these civilizations did leave behind huge monuments, such as great temples and giant statues, which tell us a lot about the history of these cultures.

TOLTECS

The Toltec civilization dominated central Mexico from 900 to 1150. In the ruined capital of Tula, today stand four massive stone statues of warriors, more than 15 feet (4.6 meters) tall, at the top of the remains of a temple. These warrior statues were a common feature of many Mesoamerican civilizations.

These warriors would once have acted as columns to hold up a higher level of the temple.

AZTECS

The Aztecs, who flourished in Mexico from the 14th to the early 16th centuries, built imposing buildings covered in monumental sculptures. Chacmools were sculptures in the shape of reclining figures, often holding a bowl or a dish. These may have been used to hold offerings for the gods.

Chacmool heads turn to the side, facing away from the offering bowl.

ART CONNECTIONS

Teotihuacán mask of obsidian, coral, and turquoise

Mesoamerican materials

Some artworks and artifacts that have survived from Mesoamerican civilizations were made from obsidian, a volcanic glasslike rock. Turquoise and colored shells were also popular materials for decorating artifacts.

49

MEDIEVAL AND RENAISSANCE ARTISTS

Artists of the medieval era were seen as skilled craftspeople, supported by powerful patrons such as nobles, royalty, and religious leaders. During the Renaissance, as more wealthy private individuals became patrons of the arts, the reputation of some artists spread far and wide, and a few even became celebrities.

UNKEI

Japanese artist Unkei brought a new realism and attention to detail to Japanese Buddhist sculpture. Some of his works stand more than 28 feet (8 meters) tall and still guard the entrances of Buddhist temples today.

c.1150–1223

RAPHAEL

A leading artist of the High Renaissance, Raphael was known for his incredibly lifelike paintings of biblical figures, characters from mythology, and important people of the day, all in rich colors.

BOTTICELLI

Working in the early Italian Renaissance, Botticelli excelled at portrait painting, for which he was much in demand among the wealthy. He also painted famous scenes from mythology.

1445–1510

1483–1520

TITIAN

A master of composition, Titian used diagonals and pyramid shapes to organize figures in his paintings. He was the leader of the Venetian Renaissance style, which favored glowing colors over line and form.

HANS HOLBEIN THE YOUNGER

Swiss German artist Holbein was one of the best portrait artists of the 16th century, as well as a printmaker. He worked at the court of King Henry VIII in England.

c.1488–1576

c.1497–1543

ARANIKO

An artist and architect from Nepal, Araniko worked under the patronage of the Chinese emperor Kublai Khan in the 13th century. His most famous project is the White Stupa in Beijing.

1245–1306

HUANG GONGWANG

An important Chinese handscroll painter of the Yuan Dynasty, Gongwang painted *Dwelling in the Fuchun Mountains*. This handscroll is nearly 23 feet (7 meters) in length.

1269–1354

JAN VAN EYCK

Building on his own work as a miniaturist painter, in the early Northern Renaissance Van Eyck mastered using oil paints to create the smallest details.

1390–1441

ANDREI RUBLEV

A painter of icons and frescoes, Rublev is considered one of the greatest artists of the Russian Orthodox Church. His biblical scenes are filled with warm, golden colors and rich jewel tones that invite deep thought and prayer.

c.1360–1430

SHIN SAIMDANG

A rare female artist working in 16th-century Korea, Saimdang is known as "Mother of the Nation" in South Korea today. Many works of embroidery, painting, and calligraphy are attributed to her.

1504–1551

LAVINIA FONTANA

Among the noblewomen in her home city of Bologna, Italy, Fontana was the most popular portrait artist. As her reputation grew, she moved to Rome, where Pope Paul V was among her famous patrons.

1552–1614

WHAT'S THE POINT OF LOOKING AT 17TH- AND 18TH-CENTURY ART?

The turbulent events of the 17th and 18th centuries led to many different directions in art. In Europe, as Christianity split into various Churches, Catholic artists created dramatic scenes of religious figures, while Protestant artists painted more everyday scenes. A series of revolutions, particularly in America and France, inspired a look back at the artistic styles of Greece and Rome, with their ancient models of democracy and empire. By contrast, a new era of peace and prosperity in Japan led artists to embrace new printing techniques that brought art to the masses.

HOW TO HONOR YOUR ANCESTORS

The islands of the Pacific Ocean, from Irian Jaya in the west to Rapa Nui in the east, were settled over thousands of years. Across the islands, there was a common belief in the ongoing presence of ancestors. Artworks ranged from small, carved items passed down through families, to ceremonial objects created for a special event. They recalled dead loved ones or leaders, and their ongoing link with the community after death.

Features were carved into a single block of stone.

MOAI OF RAPA NUI

Between the 13th and 15th centuries, more than 850 giant sculptures of enlarged, stylized heads known as *moai* were carved from stone on the island of Rapa Nui. They all face inland and are believed to represent honored ancestors.

Hei-tiki pendant, New Zealand, late 18th century

NEW ZEALAND

Among the Maori people of New Zealand, sacred pendants called *hei-tiki* typically represent a connection to a specific ancestor. Wavelike swirls carved into the face and body, known as *moko*, represent complex family histories.

Uli funeral ritual sculpture, Papua New Guinea, 18th–19th century

NEW IRELAND

Uli figures are wooden statues once created by various peoples of New Ireland in Papua New Guinea. It was believed that the spirit of a dead leader could enter the statue, where it would continue to look after the people.

War shield, Sepik River Basin, Papua New Guinea, before 1918

NEW GUINEA

The Sepik River Basin of New Guinea is home to many different cultures with similar artistic traditions. Images of animal nature spirits and human ancestors appear on objects such as masks, drums, and shields.

DID YOU KNOW?

Tau tau guardians
Since the 19th century, the Toraja people of Sulawesi in Indonesia have crafted *tau tau*. These almost life-size representations of the dead, in wood or bamboo, are created to guard tomb entrances.

Modern *tau tau* figures

HOW TO GET INTO PRINT

Japanese art and culture flourished during the Edo period (1603–1868). Illustrated books and artworks on fashionable topics such as theater or sumo were extremely popular. Printing with wooden blocks was the ideal way to mass-produce this art quickly at an affordable price, and so large printing workshops were established in major cities such as Edo (now Tokyo).

The artist drew the image with a brush.

1 Producing a woodblock print began with a publisher commissioning a design. An artist would draw the desired image in black ink on paper and provide some notes for the printer about details such as colors.

Big areas of wood that wouldn't appear in the final image were cut away with larger tools.

The detailed outline was carved out with fine tools.

DID YOU KNOW?

Ukiyo-e
Woodblock prints were known as ukiyo-e, or "pictures of the floating world." The expression "floating world" referred to the fleeting pleasures of life, such as the enjoyment of theater or the beauty of plants and landscapes.

The Great Wave, c.1830, Hokusai

2 The paper design was pasted to a block of wood. Craftspeople carved the design into the wood, creating raised lines and areas where the image would appear on the final print.

Woodblock of a design by Hiroshige

3 A printer brushed ink over the block, and the ink sat on the raised lines and areas. For multicolored prints, a separate carved block was created for each different ink color.

Paper prepared with size was hung up to dry before printing.

4 Paper was prepared with size, a gluey substance that prevents inks from running. The printer placed sized paper on the inked block and rubbed it to transfer the design to the paper.

The rubbing tool was a pad called a *baren*.

5 Finished prints were displayed to eager customers in a shop. Print publishing was a competitive business, so publishers had to watch out for current trends.

Artist
UTAGAWA HIROSHIGE

Japanese artist Hiroshige became one of the most-loved woodblock print artists of his time. His work had a poetic, human quality and he was a master at composing beautiful landscapes. He created thousands of print images, including many city scenes of Edo, and it is thought that around 10,000 prints were made from some of his print blocks.

Night View of Saruwaka Street, 1856

HOW TO INSPIRE AWE

From the 17th century, a new, often bold, style of art known as Baroque developed in Europe. It flourished in Catholic countries, where the Church set guidelines for artists in order to use art to promote their teachings. The Catholic Church thought that dramatic and powerful religious art could impress people with its authority, explain the beliefs of Catholicism, and persuade people to stay true to their faith.

Baroque sculpture

Religious sculptures were detailed, ornamental, and full of movement. This sense of movement was created by swirling folds of fabric and twisting, dynamic poses.

The Ecstasy of St. Teresa, 1645–1652, Gian Lorenzo Bernini

Appearing from a burst of bright, heavenly light above makes the angel an impressive figure.

POWER AND GLORY

Artists of the Catholic Baroque painted religious scenes to make viewers feel moved and amazed by the divine power of God and the Church. One popular subject was angels appearing to awestruck characters from the Bible.

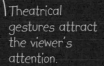
Theatrical gestures attract the viewer's attention.

Artist
ARTEMISIA GENTILESCHI

Italian Baroque painter Gentileschi achieved great success during an era when there were very few female artists. She painted scenes from religion and myth, while other women mostly painted portraits, which were seen as less ambitious. The style that she developed was startlingly bold and realistic and often showed strong female characters.

ADDING DRAMA

Artists chose dramatic scenes and approaches to get their message across and draw viewers in. Many Baroque artists used action, emotion, exaggerated poses, close-ups, unusual angles, and lighting effects to do this.

The Supper at Emmaus, 1601, Caravaggio

Scenes often have just one source of light.

LET THERE BE LIGHT

Painters used strong contrasts of light and dark in a technique known as "chiaroscuro" (Italian for "bright-dark"). The effect created drama and suggested God's divine light. Italian painter Caravaggio led the way in this technique.

Self-Portrait as the Allegory of Painting, c.1638–1639

THE DUTCH GOLDEN AGE

The Dutch region (known today as the Netherlands) saw a "golden age" of wealth and power in the 17th century, and art flourished. Rather than the dramatic religious art of Catholic countries, the art of this Protestant region reflected people's everyday experiences. The many middle-class Dutch art-buyers favored these subjects but liked typical Baroque light-and-shade effects.

Girl with a Pearl Earring, c.1665, Johannes Vermeer

PORTRAITS

Growing numbers of successful Dutch businesspeople wanted pictures of themselves or their relations to hang at home. Portraits were often natural, direct, and informal rather than stiff and posed.

STILL LIFES

The Dutch loved still-life paintings, such as arrangements of fruit or flowers, even though the art world often looked down on them as too ordinary. To the Dutch, beautiful still lifes reflected their nation's success and the bounty of nature.

A messy table adds everyday realism.

Artist REMBRANDT

Dutch artist Rembrandt's work ranged from self-portraits that were very realistic for the time, to large, dramatic paintings such as *The Night Watch*, which shows soldiers guarding the city of Amsterdam. He was a master of light effects.

The Night Watch, 1642

EVERYDAY FOLK

Dutch Golden Age artists didn't just focus on showing grand people or religious characters. Kitchen maids, musicians, and other ordinary people going about their day were featured prominently in many paintings.

Landscape paintings had atmospheric sky and light effects.

LANDSCAPES

Before the 17th century, landscapes were usually just a background for another subject. Skilled Dutch artists helped promote the landscape as a worthy topic for entire paintings in its own right.

Including the family dog gives a cozy, natural feel.

GENRE PAINTING

A category of art known as genre painting features subjects from daily life. Dutch artists specialized in relaxed, informal (and sometimes chaotic) scenes of places such as homes and taverns.

HOW TO BE THEATRICAL

Reacting against the strong colors and serious drama of Baroque art, Rococo artists in the 18th century wanted to give their art a light, soft, playful feel. Rococo featured detailed, exaggerated decoration, and elegance and luxury were important. It was popular in France, where paintings often showed aristocrats enjoying lighthearted pastimes in a theatrical way.

STRIKING A POSE

Rococo art shows rich people wearing fancy, artificial-looking clothes, often striking theatrical poses. They stand in ways that *seem exaggerated now*, but which at the time were thought to be elegant and refined.

An emphasis on luxury appears in clothing details, such as velvet collars and lace cuffs.

GRACEFUL CURVES

Rococo styles are filled with curves. This reflects a love of shapes taken from nature, such as shells. The word "Rococo" probably comes from the French *rocaille*, a type of decoration using shells and pebbles.

INSPIRED BY NATURE

Detailed decorations inspired by nature covered everything in Rococo art. Grand fountains were a common feature of paintings, and were decorated with animals, plantlike shapes, and aquatic scenes.

Flowers are shown everywhere—real ones and also floral designs.

Pastel colors were especially popular.

Artist
JEAN-HONORÉ FRAGONARD

French artist Fragonard made some of the most typical and best-loved Rococo-style paintings, such as *The Swing*. He spent time in Italy, and its art and landscape influenced the free feel and soft colors of his paintings. Fragonard's romantic, amusing scenes shimmer with light, while skillful, lively brushstrokes make delicately glowing colors stand out against each other.

FÊTES GALANTES

Scenes of elegant parties taking place in the countryside, parkland, or lush gardens were very popular in Rococo art. These parties—and the paintings showing them—are often called fêtes galantes ("courtship parties").

The Swing, c.1767–1768

HOW TO ACHIEVE HARMONY

In Europe, during the later 18th and early 19th centuries, many artists reacted against the lighthearted Rococo style by making work that was more serious. They were inspired by ancient Greece and Rome—the classical civilizations—and their ideals of virtue and harmony. Artists aimed to revive these ideals in their own way, and their style came to be called Neoclassicism ("neo" means "new").

It was fashionable to include classical buildings and people in paintings.

CLASSICAL INFLUENCE

Two factors made classical values popular. First, the earlier much-loved art of French 17th-century artists Nicolas Poussin and Claude showed classical order and harmony. Second, in the 18th century, the ancient cities of Herculaneum and Pompeii were unearthed, sparking an interest in ancient Roman civilization.

Ancient Greek and Roman thinkers promoted moral virtues, such as self-sacrifice.

ENLIGHTENMENT VALUES

A period and movement closely linked to Neoclassical art was "The Enlightenment," or "Age of Reason." With strong roots in classical ideas, it promoted the idea that reason and clear thought brought knowledge, tolerance, and well-being. Artists tried to bring these values into their work.

Artist
JACQUES-LOUIS DAVID

French artist David was greatly influenced by classical art and ideas—for example, the belief that reason could bring about social changes. Such ideas led to the French Revolution (1787–1799), after which David became the favorite artist of France's new ruler, Napoleon Bonaparte.

WELL-ORDERED IMAGES

Just as classical buildings have simple, symmetrical (evenly balanced), clear forms, Neoclassical artists aimed to arrange the items in their paintings in the same way. Their arrangements often follow simple, strong, straight lines such as triangles.

Napoleon Crossing the Alps, 1800

65

17TH- AND 18TH-CENTURY ARTISTS

Catholic artists of the 17th and early 18th centuries, particularly in Italy and Spain, produced many rich and dramatic religious works. In Protestant northern Europe and the American colonies, artists tended to create more subdued works that were less focused on religion. This period saw a few famous female artists and the birth of a new printmaking tradition in Japan.

CARAVAGGIO

With his dramatic use of light and dark, Caravaggio was the star of Italian Baroque painting. He painted realistically and did not try to idealize his figures.

1571–1610

CANALETTO

Italian artist Canaletto is famous for his detailed vistas of famous Italian cities and landmarks. Wealthy people on grand tours of Europe would purchase a Canaletto painting as a souvenir.

1697–1768

RACHEL RUYSCH

During the Baroque period, when Dutch people were moving away from dramatic religious art toward lifelike paintings, Ruysch excelled at detailed still-life paintings of flowers.

1664–1750

JOHN SINGLETON COPLEY

The first famous American artist, Copley had to earn his living in England rather than in his homeland, where there were no art schools or museums yet.

1738–1815

ADÉLAÏDE LABILLE-GUIARD

A French painter, Labille-Guiard was admitted to the French Académie Royale when only four female painters were allowed at a time. Beyond producing her own works, she trained the next generation of female painters in France.

1749–1803

PETER-PAUL RUBENS

Capturing the drama and excitement of the Flemish Baroque style, the most famous paintings of Rubens are large and colorful, often showing gods or saints in epic battles.

1577–1640

DIEGO VELÁZQUEZ

Skilled at painting everyday scenes, such as busy taverns or small groups of people at home, Velázquez also portrayed the rich surroundings of the court of King Phillip IV of Spain.

1599–1660

VERMEER

Superstar of the Dutch Baroque, Vermeer is known for quiet indoor scenes with sunlight streaming through the windows. Household objects were symbols for deeper emotions.

1632–1675

JUDITH LEYSTER

At a time when few women worked as artists, Leyster was a successful painter of the Dutch Baroque. Many of her works are scenes of everyday life with jolly musicians.

1609–1660

ÉLISABETH VIGÉE LE BRUN

Madame Le Brun was a successful French artist despite her lack of a formal art education. She served as the portrait painter to Marie-Antoinette, Queen of France.

1755–1842

HOKUSAI

Prints of Hokusaï's work were created using a Japanese woodblock printing technique that was popular at this time. These prints featured bold areas of color and simple black outlines.

1760–1849

WHAT'S THE POINT OF LOOKING AT 19TH-CENTURY ART?

Life in Europe and America modernized quickly in the 19th century. Factories brought more people to live in dirty, crowded cities, so artists depicted the tough lives of the poor for the first time. Some artists believed factories removed the creative element from the production process, and started to make their own unique, handcrafted designs. The invention of photography also had a great influence on artists. Some embraced its ability to capture a fleeting moment. Others saw the realism of photography as a reason to embrace less lifelike techniques in painting—paving the way for more abstract styles of modern art.

HOW TO BRING THE DRAMA

European society underwent a period of great change from the late 18th to the mid-19th century. This was reflected in the arts by a revolutionary movement called Romanticism, which spread across much of western Europe. Artists of the Romantic movement celebrated passion, imagination, and the wild power of nature in their works. They created powerful art that stirred people to think, feel, dream, and wonder.

Medieval Gothic ruins often featured in Romantic works. Gothic architecture was associated with the supernatural in Romantic art and literature.

NATURE'S POWER

The Romantics were fascinated by the sublime—a feeling of awe and fear, which could be inspired by the natural world. Scenes of extreme weather, shipwrecks, and natural disasters demonstrated nature's power, creating intense feelings of terror and wonder in the viewer.

A REVOLUTIONARY WORLD

Uprisings in France and America led to deadly conflicts, and Romantic artists sympathized with ordinary people in their fight for freedom and equality. In their dramatic depictions of revolution, artists conveyed strong feelings of patriotism, honor, loss, and sacrifice.

The Third of May 1808, 1814, Francisco Goya

DRAMATIC LANDSCAPES

Landscape painting became popular in the 19th century. In the US, artists of the Hudson River School were inspired by the American wilderness with its wide-open spaces, beautiful vistas, and unknown territories.

Rocky Mountain Landscape, 1870, Albert Bierstadt

THE INDIVIDUAL

Being true to the thoughts and feelings of the individual was important for the Romantics. Solitary figures in art could represent people opening themselves up to inner feelings or connecting deeply to nature.

Artists found inspiration in cultures to the east of Europe, which were thought of as exotic. But these artists often knew very little about the real people or places of these far-off lands.

Artist
CASPAR DAVID FRIEDRICH

The most influential German Romantic landscape artist, Friedrich had a difficult, tragic childhood, which brought a lonely and sombre quality to his paintings. He was deeply religious, and his works represented nature as an expression of God's power. He liked to depict people from behind, inviting us into his works so that we feel—like his figures— alone in nature's grandeur.

The Wanderer above the Sea of Fog, c.1818

HOW TO KEEP THINGS REAL

In the mid-19th century, a group of artists in France grew tired of creating idealized or romanticized scenes featuring beautiful or important people. Instead, they focused on showing realistic scenes of modern life, such as workers in the country and the city, local landscapes, and portraits of ordinary people. This major movement, known as Realism, was influential throughout Europe and the US.

WORKING PEOPLE

Realist artists showed ordinary working people as they really looked, doing hard jobs such as breaking stones along roads or working in the fields. When these artworks were exhibited in galleries, many visitors were shocked to see such people in paintings.

Faces are realistic and not idealized.

Clothes are dirty, torn, and tatty.

Artist
GUSTAVE COURBET

Rebellious French artist Courbet had great compassion for ordinary working people. He showed their lives in powerful, highly realistic paintings and addressed social issues, which caused a stir among many viewers. However, Courbet was very influential and is seen as the leader of Realism.

Peasants of Flagey Returning from the Fair, 1850–1855

PORTRAITS

Realists rejected the idea that portraits must show grand people in fine surroundings. Instead, they often painted their friends and relatives in everyday settings. The coloring was often plain and subdued.

Poses were natural, rather than stiff and formal, perhaps turned away as if caught in a chance moment.

Émile Zola, 1868, painting by Édouard Manet

The highlights on the trousers are believable, but loose brushwork adds the artist's own individual touch.

Émile Zola, 1880s/1890s, photo by Studio Nadar

The camera has caught highlights in a way that creates great contrasts of light and dark.

PHOTOGRAPHY

The invention and advancement of photography in the 19th century had a big influence on artists. For example, because photography could capture life in very realistic ways, Realists were free to focus on their subject matter instead of on trying to copy what a camera could do.

73

HOW TO CAPTURE THE MOMENT

Invented in the 1820s, photography is a relatively young technology, but it has developed into an important art form. Photography records a permanent image by focusing light on a light-sensitive surface. It is particularly suited to capturing the real world, documenting life as it happens. Artists have used photography to capture historic moments, to record the state of society, and to send a political message.

Early photographers covered their heads to block out light and see the image they were photographing more easily.

People posing for photographs had to stand very still because the exposure time (how long it took the camera to collect light) was several minutes long.

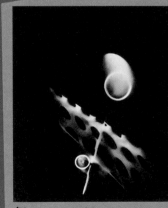

Photogram, 1925, László Moholy-Nagy

Abstract photography
Starting in the early 20th century, artists experimented with cameras and light-sensitive paper to create artistic effects. The images were abstract—they didn't focus on recognizable people or objects.

WAR PHOTOGRAPHY

One of the first documentary uses of photography was to record the day-to-day lives of soldiers in the US Civil War. Photographers were unable to capture the action of a battle because early cameras took too long to create the image, but today's cameras can capture moments of violence that highlight the horrors of war.

STREET PHOTOGRAPHY

Taking a snapshot in seconds allows photographers to capture the real hustle and bustle of a busy city block. Street photography is usually candid (truthful and informal) and neutral in its depiction of the world, though photographers often focus on marginalized groups and the places they live and work in.

Street photographers celebrate the energy and movement of a particular time and place.

A photojournalist's picture of a disaster can often be more powerful than a written article.

PHOTOJOURNALISM

From the 1920s, when cameras became faster and lighter, photographers were able to take photos to illustrate news stories. Photojournalists often travel to dangerous places to capture the latest news, and their powerful images of events can be seen by millions just minutes later.

Artist
ANSEL ADAMS

Adams specialized in photographing the American wilderness and was very skilled at capturing beautiful compositions, mainly in black and white. He was an early environmental campaigner, and used his art to document the natural world and highlight the importance of preserving the wilderness.

The Tetons and the Snake River, 1942

HOW TO CREATE AN IMPRESSION

In the late 19th century, the Impressionists—a group of mainly French artists—rebelled against "proper" art. Refusing to paint detailed scenes from history and myth, they revolutionized art by using rapid strokes to capture immediate, personal impressions of everyday modern life and changing weather and light conditions.

EN PLEIN AIR

Artists traditionally made sketches outside and slowly turned these into paintings in a studio. But Impressionists such as Claude Monet quickly created a scene in paint *en plein air* (French for "in the open air"), carrying tubes of paint and a folding easel—recent inventions at the time.

Artist
BERTHE MORISOT

An expert at portraying the everyday lives of women, Morisot painted at a time when it was hard for women to be accepted as artists. Early outdoor painting experiences helped her develop sparkling light effects, made with fast, loose brushstrokes.

Young Woman Knitting, c.1883

LIGHT

The Impressionists wanted to record fleeting light effects accurately before they vanished. For example, Pierre-Auguste Renoir captured dappled (patchy) light and shade across a scene, painting shadows with colors rather than black or gray.

Dance at Le Moulin de la Galette, 1876, Pierre-Auguste Renoir

Renoir showed the shifting, dappled shade created by light shining through trees.

ART CONNECTIONS

Photographic impressions

The rapidly advancing art of photography was an influence on the Impressionists. They were struck by how a photo could freeze a particular moment, cutting off a scene at the edges—an effect used in Impressionist painting.

Tree Study, Forest of Fontainebleau, c.1856, Gustave Le Gray

Fascinated by movement, Degas sketched dancers over and over again.

NEW VIEWPOINTS

Catching ordinary moments from unusual angles was pioneered by the Impressionists. Edgar Degas often showed dancers resting or rehearsing rather than performing, with some dancers facing away from the viewer.

POSTIMPRESSIONISM

From roughly the 1880s to the early 1900s, various artists built on—or reacted against—the Impressionists' experiments with natural light and color. They had very different styles but are often grouped together as the Postimpressionists. Painters such as Georges Seurat, Paul Cezanne, and Vincent van Gogh pushed art in all kinds of new directions that helped pave the way for other modern styles that came next.

Small dashes and dots of different colors look like solid shapes and blended color when seen from a distance.

Georges Seurat

PAINTING WITH DOTS

French artist Georges Seurat was fascinated by the science of color. He pioneered a technique called Pointillism. Close up, you see tiny painted dots of very different colors. Stand back and your eye and brain "mix" them to look realistic. This is called "optical mixing."

A Sunday on La Grande Jatte—1884, 1884–1886, Georges Seurat

EXPRESSIVE BRUSHSTROKES

The works of Dutch artist Vincent van Gogh are painted rapidly with "impasto"—applying paint thickly so that the brushstrokes are visible. His aim was to express powerful emotions rather than to create realistic scenes.

The Starry Night, 1889, Vincent van Gogh

Thick paint and obvious brushstrokes make us aware that we are looking at a painting.

Paul Cezanne

Vincent van Gogh

The fruit is built up with geometric shapes and little color patches that suggest different angles.

SHAPES AND ANGLES

French painter Paul Cezanne painted a natural world that was based on what he believed were its underlying geometric shapes, such as spheres and cones. His unusual angles mirror how we see the world from different angles at the same time, and his work later became an influence on abstract art.

Mont Sainte-Victoire, 1902–1904, Paul Cezanne

79

HOW TO RESPECT YOUR MATERIALS

From the mid-19th century, a group of English artists and designers became highly critical of what they saw as low-quality items created in factories. They formed the Arts and Crafts movement, which wanted to return to traditional crafting methods. Members valued hand-crafted "honesty"—making objects from ordinary materials in a way that showed their quality. The movement, pioneered by designer William Morris, spread to the rest of Europe and the US.

Furniture was made to be solidly built, practical, and beautiful.

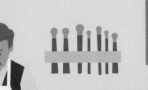

Simpler designs were usually preferred to fussy ones.

FURNITURE

Craftspeople wanted to stay true to their materials. In England, they chose native English woods for furniture—especially oak—and often gave it a simple, natural finish instead of covering it with thick stains.

Artist
WILLIAM MORRIS

English designer and writer Morris was a leading Arts and Crafts figure. He and his wife couldn't find furnishings they liked for their home, so they and some friends produced their own. Morris and others founded a company in 1861, and his designs are still admired today.

Detail of *Bird* design (1878) on wool wall hanging

Inspired by nature, Morris's beautifully detailed designs featured different kinds of plants.

Blocks were tapped with a mallet to transfer the design evenly.

Architecture

Arts and Crafts buildings looked natural and organic. To achieve this, architects used local materials and asymmetrical layouts, with features such as uneven roofs.

Red House, Bexleyheath, England, 1859–1860, Philip Webb

PRINTS

Arts and Crafts designers believed in tradition and natural materials. Most of the wallpapers and printed fabrics made by William Morris's company were printed by hand, using hand-carved wooden blocks and natural dyes.

Morris's company made tapestries and carpets on large, hand-operated looms.

DID YOU KNOW?

Rose Valley

In the US, Arts and Crafts ideas appealed to the American "back to nature" pioneer spirit. Various artists' communities sprang up, such as Rose Valley in Philadelphia, which made furniture, metalwork, and pottery.

Library table (Rose Valley), 1904, William Lightfoot Price

WOVEN TEXTILES

William Morris created Arts and Crafts versions of the great medieval tapestries he loved, showcasing their rich colors and detail. Morris also produced other textiles such as carpets and curtains.

HOW TO GO WITH THE FLOW

In the late 19th and early 20th centuries, many artists in Europe and the US, tired of what they saw as old-fashioned approaches to art, created the style of Art Nouveau—"new art" in French. Art Nouveau took inspiration from recent trends in art, combining the flowing lines of Japanese prints with nature-based designs from movements such as Arts and Crafts.

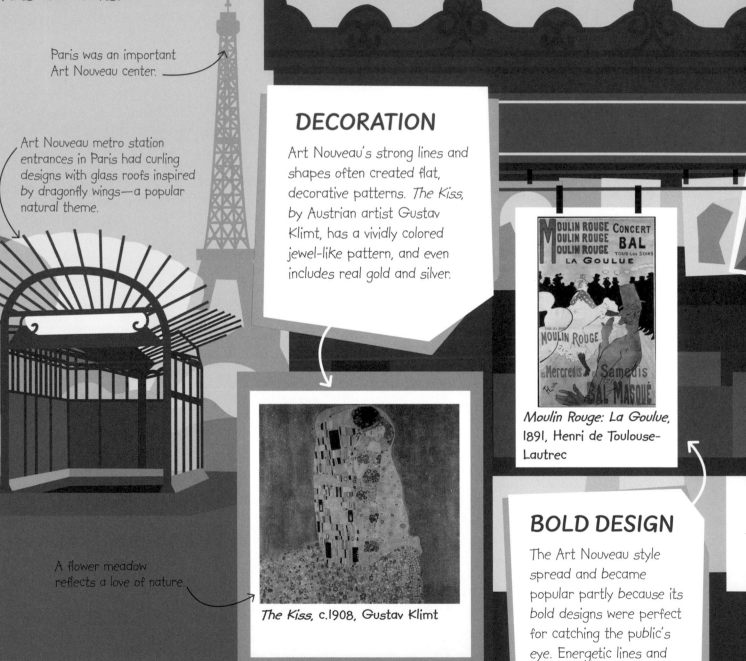

Paris was an important Art Nouveau center.

Art Nouveau metro station entrances in Paris had curling designs with glass roofs inspired by dragonfly wings—a popular natural theme.

DECORATION

Art Nouveau's strong lines and shapes often created flat, decorative patterns. *The Kiss*, by Austrian artist Gustav Klimt, has a vividly colored jewel-like pattern, and even includes real gold and silver.

Moulin Rouge: La Goulue, 1891, Henri de Toulouse-Lautrec

A flower meadow reflects a love of nature.

The Kiss, c.1908, Gustav Klimt

BOLD DESIGN

The Art Nouveau style spread and became popular partly because its bold designs were perfect for catching the public's eye. Energetic lines and bright colors brought advertising posters to life.

Across the arts

Art Nouveau artists gave equal value to all art and craft forms. The style was seen in buildings, furniture, glasswork, vases, and jewelry. French designer René Lalique produced striking Art Nouveau jewelry.

"Female Face" pendant, c.1900, René Lalique

The newspaper kiosks of early 20th-century Paris were covered in Art Nouveau advertising images.

The Peacock Skirt, 1890s, Aubrey Beardsley

Sarah Bernhardt, 1897, Alphonse Mucha

ILLUSTRATION

The public enjoyed seeing the Art Nouveau style in book and magazine illustrations. In English artist Aubrey Beardsley's illustrations, powerful compositions and a lack of depth and symmetry show the influence of Japanese prints.

CURVING LINES

Long, curling women's hair was often featured because it created elegantly curving, flowing lines. Czech artist Alphonse Mucha was the master of Art Nouveau posters, especially those promoting the actress Sarah Bernhardt.

19TH-CENTURY ARTISTS

Artists of the 19th century were influenced by a world that was transforming around them. As the Industrial Revolution spread from Britain and revolts and rebellions attempted to bring great political changes, artists split into many different schools and movements. Romantics painted drama, Realists showed the hardworking poor, and Impressionists captured fleeting moments.

FRANCISCO DE GOYA

Spanish painter de Goya worked in the Romantic style. He put candles in his hat so that he could paint at night. De Goya didn't shy away from violent, nightmarish imagery in some of his works.

1746–1828

AUGUSTE RODIN

French sculptor Rodin produced some of the first major modern works of sculpture. Rather than the typical heroic generals on horseback, he produced works like *The Thinker*— a seated man deep in thought.

HARRIET POWERS

African American artist Powers created quilts. Instead of using typical quilting patterns, her designs featured stories inspired by her time in enslavement before its abolition in the US.

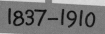
1837–1910

1840–1917

CLAUDE MONET

An Impressionist painter from France, Monet was interested in light and atmosphere. He often painted the same landscape at different times of day and year, capturing different colors.

MARY CASSATT

American Impressionist Cassatt lived in Paris, France. She concentrated on indoor scenes of women and children, because that was the world she was most familiar with.

1840–1926

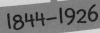
1844–1926

JOHN CONSTABLE

Working at a time when factories and machines started appearing in England, British artist Constable painted sun-dappled scenes of the countryside, focusing on rural subjects that were in danger of disappearing.

EUGÈNE DELACROIX

A Romantic painter from France, Delacroix created dramatic scenes of war and struggle. His works also showed a fascination with faraway cultures and different ways of life.

1776–1837

1798–1863

JEAN-FRANÇOIS MILLET

French painter Millet championed the style of Realism. His scenes of rural peasant life were not what people expected to see in art galleries.

ÉDOUARD MANET

French painter Manet broke from convention to follow Realist ideas and paint ordinary scenes of city life. An Impressionist, he painted with rapid, loose brushstrokes and patches of color.

1814–1875

1832–1883

VINCENT VAN GOGH

Post-Impressionist Dutch painter Van Gogh rejected realism in favor of self-expression. He used vibrant oil colors painted with very visible brushstrokes to provoke an emotional reaction in the viewer.

EDMONIA LEWIS

Sculptor Lewis had African American and Native American parents. Her sculptures often featured figures from these ethnic backgrounds, which was unusual compared to mainstream art of the day.

1844–1907

1853–1890

85

WHAT'S THE POINT OF LOOKING AT
MODERN ART?

Artists of the early and mid-20th century were rebels and rule breakers.
They pushed the limits of art, using unusual materials and methods, so
much so that they were sometimes called animals in the newspapers.
Abstract art was born at this time—at its most extreme, this was art
without a subject, formed of just colors and shapes. Some artists used
anything they could find to create their art: a bicycle wheel, a collage of
photos, or objects that had been thrown away. The things they made
were meant to challenge our ideas about and expectations of art,
and they still do today.

HOW TO EXPRESS YOURSELF

In the late 19th and early 20th centuries, many European artists reacted against styles that aimed to be "realistic." They chose instead to show the world through personal expression of their own emotions. This led to several different art movements, as some artists used characters and scenes to stand for internal feelings, while others used exaggeration or vivid colors to portray their inner life.

SYMBOLISM

Some artists expressed the hidden worlds they found behind outward appearances by using symbols—images that can represent ideas and emotions in complicated ways. They often created a powerful, emotional mood rather than just telling a straightforward story.

Death symbols included cloaked skeleton figures based on ancient myth.

DID YOU KNOW?

The Scream
The garish colors and swirling lines in Edvard Munch's Symbolist painting *The Scream* express the Norwegian artist's great personal anxiety. The close links between its style and subject make this an early influence on Expressionism.

The Scream, c.1910, Edvard Munch

Objects are often highly simplified in Expressionist paintings.

EXPRESSIONISM

Sending a powerful emotional message was the most important thing for Expressionist artists. They painted strange worlds in odd colors that were full of unexpected angles and exaggerated features.

FAUVISM

The French Fauvists rejected tradition and experimented with intense, unnatural colors and simplified shapes to express their feelings. "Fauve" is French for "wild beast," which is how a critic described them at the time.

Artist
HENRI MATISSE

Because of his original use of bold colors, French artist Matisse is often seen as the main Fauvist. He was influenced by Impressionism, but his paintings ended up using more unusual colors and forms. When he became ill in later life and painting was too difficult, Matisse made colorful images from shapes cut out of brightly painted paper.

The Fauvists loved painting landscapes, but their colors were far from natural.

TRY IT OUT
PLAYING WITH COLORS

Create a Fauvist picture of your favorite landscape with colored pencils or paints. Instead of the colors you would usually use, pick different, "unrealistic" ones. How has using these colors changed how you feel about your picture?

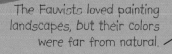

Icarus, 1947

HOW TO SEE LIFE FROM ALL ANGLES

In 1907, Spanish artist Pablo Picasso and French artist Georges Braque went to an exhibition of the works of Paul Cezanne (see pages 78–79). Inspired by how Cezanne broke down reality into geometric shapes, Picasso and Braque took this further—they wanted to separate out how the human eye sees objects in time and space. The result was the influential art movement known as Cubism.

1 Braque liked to experiment with perspective. To achieve this, he walked around the objects he painted to capture them from different viewpoints. Braque thought that any sort of objects, no matter how everyday, could be used to make art.

DID YOU KNOW?

African art influences
In Picasso's Cubist portraits, he simplifies forms, often taking inspiration from African tribal masks that are stylized rather than realistic. Picasso kept a large collection of African masks in his studio while he worked.

African tribal mask

2 With Cezanne's work in mind, Braque set out to challenge the tradition of painting objects realistically. He broke down objects into simple geometric shapes, such as cubes, circles, and triangles.

3 Braque's painting *The Round Table* (1929) shows objects seen from different angles and simplified to their most basic shapes to create a flat image. Later Cubist paintings were even more fragmented.

Artist
PABLO PICASSO

One of the most important artists of the 20th century, Spanish painter Picasso was a pioneer of several different art movements and styles but is perhaps best known as a founder of Cubism. During his long life, Picasso was amazingly prolific, producing more than 20,000 artworks, from paintings and sculptures to ballet costumes and set designs.

TRY IT OUT
CUBIST COLLAGE

Make your own Cubist collage. Paint or photograph an object from different angles. Then tear up the paintings or photos, arrange the pieces in an interesting way, and stick them onto paper. Do you prefer the "realistic" artwork or the Cubist version?

Pitcher

 +

Torn out pieces of printouts

Finished collage

Weeping Woman, 1937

HOW TO FIND ART ANYWHERE

The horrors of World War I made the art world seem absurd to some artists, who founded the Dada movement in 1915 to shake things up. They created shocking works that often seemed nonsensical. Artists sometimes made use of found objects—ordinary objects that you might find anywhere—and presented them as art. Found object art outlasted the Dada movement, and can still be seen today in some conceptual art, in which ideas are more important than the physical artwork.

2 The artist carefully photographs the pile so that she has an accurate record of each object's position. Then other people help the artist carefully dismantle the pile and take all the objects away.

Part of what appeals to the artist is the random way in which the objects are muddled up.

1 Walking along a beach, an artist finds a pile of washed-up objects. She thinks it will make a stimulating artwork because of the objects' shapes and textures and because they represent ideas about seaside environments.

WHAT IS ART?

Are found objects art?

Some people think that found objects can't be art because they haven't been made from scratch by the artist. Others believe that anything that stimulates an artist can be called art. What do you think?

God (plumbing trap on wooden miter box), c.1917, Elsa von Freytag-Loringhoven

3 To use this new artwork in her latest exhibition, the artist assembles the pile of objects again in the art gallery, on a small plinth (platform). The artwork is roped off so that people cannot damage or disturb the objects.

The artist has made sure that the pile looks as close to how she found it as possible.

Artist
MARCEL DUCHAMP

French artist Duchamp *believed* that an ordinary object could become a piece of art if an artist said it was. Duchamp wanted to make people think about what an artwork was. He is said to have invented the idea of the "ready-made"—a found object that is an everyday, mass-produced object presented as art.

TRY IT OUT
RECYCLED ART

Some artists work with objects or materials that had a certain purpose but are no longer being used. Their work often makes a point about how these items were originally used, or their disposable nature. Using objects around your home, try making a piece of art that expresses what you think about the environment.

Bicycle Wheel (assisted ready-made of bicycle wheel and stool), 1913

HOW TO BE ABSTRACT

The modern world was changing quickly in the early 20th century, and artists were looking for new ideas to match that change. Some broke away from tradition and made art that was abstract—it didn't look like anything from the world around us. Abstract artists believed that lines, shapes, and colors created a different kind of reality that was worthy in its own right.

Non-Objective Composition (Suprematism), 1916, Olga Rozanova

SUPREMATISM

In 1915, Russian artist Kazimir Malevich founded Suprematism, a movement that pioneered an extreme abstract style. Malevich thought it was more important to create work that accessed pure, deep meaning than to show recognizable objects. Russian artist Olga Rozanova was also part of the Suprematist movement.

Artist
VASILY KANDINSKY

Around 1913, Russian-born artist Kandinsky made some of the West's earliest totally abstract art. He gave pictures musical titles because he compared abstract art to music and thought that both could express spiritual feelings.

Composition 8, 1923

Composition C (No. III) with Red, Yellow, and Blue, 1935, Piet Mondrian

BAUHAUS

The Bauhaus was a German school of art and design, famous for a simple, bold, geometric style that greatly influenced modern and abstract art. It taught students that all kinds of art and technical crafts, from painting to metalwork, had equal value.

Bauhaus exhibition poster design, 1923, Joost Schmidt

DE STIJL

Dutch for "The Style," De Stijl was a Dutch art movement founded in 1917. Members of the group, such as Piet Mondrian, strove for a very ordered, geometric, abstract harmony that could be applied to life as well as art. Mondrian used blocks of primary colors in geometric grids.

ART CONNECTIONS

Bauhaus school
The German word "Bauhaus" translates as "house of building." Architect Walter Gropius, the school's German American founder, believed that architecture brought together many different types of art.

Bauhaus school, Dessau, built 1925–1926 from designs by Walter Gropius

HOW TO PAINT A DREAM

Starting in Europe during the 1920s, a group of writers, thinkers, and artists called the Surrealists questioned accepted ideas about the real world and its logic. Instead, they turned to their own dreams and unconscious minds to find new, startling truths. Many Surrealist artists showed realistic objects or scenes in ways that seemed strange or impossible. The name Surrealism comes from French words that mean "super reality."

REAL AND UNREAL

The Surrealists liked to mix the real with the unreal. German-Swiss artist Meret Oppenheim covered an ordinary cup, saucer, and spoon with fur to show us a different kind of reality.

Object, 1936, Meret Oppenheim

TIME TO DREAM

Spanish Surrealist Salvador Dalí found his creative ideas by letting himself go into a dreamlike state. He was fascinated by time, and *The Persistence of Memory* shows a dream landscape that explores ideas of time and the nature of memory.

The Persistence of Memory, 1931, Salvador Dalí

Surrealist artists often presented everyday objects in surprising ways.

The Son of Man, 1964, René Magritte

HIDE AND SEEK

Surrealism is full of symbols and hidden meanings. Belgian artist René Magritte said that *The Son of Man* was a self-portrait, but the man's face is mostly hidden by an apple. He believed that what we could see was always hiding something else.

TRY IT OUT
AUTOMATIC DRAWING

Some artists linked with Surrealism, such as the Spanish artist Joan Miró, used a technique called automatic drawing, or automatism. They aimed to draw or paint freely to make art directly from their unconscious minds. Try this yourself and see where your pencil, pen, or brush takes you— make sure you don't think about what you are doing!

HOW TO PAINT AN AMERICAN SCENE

Since the birth of the US in 1776, American artists have struggled to create their own unique style of art. In the 20th century, as more abstract styles were emerging in Europe, artists in the US moved in the opposite direction, depicting American cities, landscapes, and scenes of everyday life.

Regionalists celebrated their homeland by painting a simple barn or a field of grain.

THE ASHCAN SCHOOL

In the early 1900s, a loose group of artists, fed up with the more refined subjects they saw in American art, began to paint the gritty reality of poorer New York neighborhoods, from street scenes to working-class entertainments (such as boxing).

REGIONALISM

Between the two world wars, a group of painters known as the Regionalists wanted to create art that praised everyday American lives. They rejected city scenes and romanticized American rural landscapes and people.

American Gothic, 1930, Grant Wood

AMERICANA

Norman Rockwell was a Regionalist whose illustrations appeared in *Saturday Evening Post* magazine from 1916 to 1963. His extremely popular art was filled with wholesome scenes of small-town America with its diners and baseball fields.

Rockwell's art often featured children at the center of the scene.

URBAN LIVES

While Regionalists concentrated on rural America, Edward Hopper captured the isolation of living in a bustling American city. His paintings have an eerie quality that shows how people can be lonely even when they are not alone.

Artist
GEORGIA O'KEEFFE

In the 1920s, O'Keeffe became an important American artist when very few women could do so. She was influenced by new abstract styles arriving from Europe, and her works often have an abstract quality. O'Keeffe's art celebrates different aspects of American life, from towering city skyscrapers to delicate desert flowers of the American Southwest.

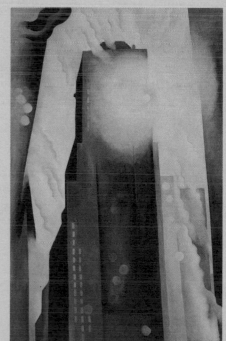

The Shelton with Sunspots, N.Y., 1926

HOW TO BE SPONTANEOUS

Based in New York in the 1940s and 1950s, the Abstract Expressionists made large, abstract works that expressed their emotions. They believed in free creativity, and wanted to produce art that came from the unconscious mind. Although their art appeared purely spontaneous (created on impulse), elements of the work were carefully planned.

NO MAIN FOCUS

Traditional paintings often guided the viewer's eye to a particular area of the canvas. However, Abstract Expressionist paintings often had no main focus.

QUICK PAINTING

Despite frequently using rapid techniques to express energy and freedom, artists often controlled the processes carefully and thoughtfully.

ACTION PAINTING

Some Abstract Expressionists' work is called "Action Painting." This reflects an approach where artists were closely involved physically with the paint and the moment of painting—perhaps moving quickly around a canvas on the floor, or making a wild, huge sweep with a brush.

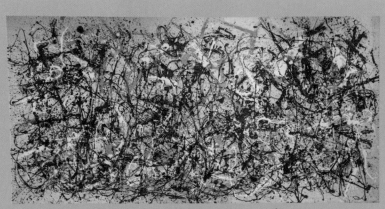

Autumn Rhythm (Number 30), 1950, Jackson Pollock

Looking down from above gave a new, different perspective compared to working on an easel.

LARGE CANVAS

Works were often very large, making dramatic statements. American artist Jackson Pollock placed huge, untreated canvases on the floor, then walked around and on them. For his "drip paintings," he poured, dribbled, and flicked paint from above.

Artists often chose to use paints meant for houses or cars rather than artists' paints.

LOTS OF PAINT

Being expressive was helped by using plenty of liquid paint, instead of mixing small amounts of artists' paint on a palette. Jackson Pollock would literally pour paint directly from a can!

COLOR FIELD

Works that were called "Color Field" art were usually large canvases with a huge field (area) of color. Typically, the idea was to have very little surface detail. Works often seemed calm and they focused on how the viewer perceived color.

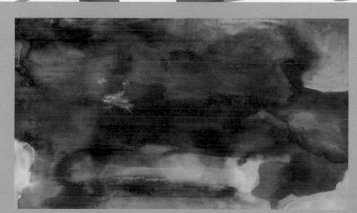

Riverhead, 1963, Helen Frankenthaler

EARLY 20TH-CENTURY ARTISTS

Many artists of the early 20th century experimented with abstract art—painting with pure lines, shapes, and color, without representing things from the real world. Though this idea has always existed in art, it broke new ground at this time.

HILMA AF KLINT

Not widely known during her lifetime, Swedish artist Af Klint has gained international fame for her pioneering abstract paintings, created years before abstract art received great attention from other artists.

1862–1944

DOROTHEA LANGE

During the Great Depression, American photographer Lange captured heartbreaking moments of poverty and despair among workers and farmers. Some of her photographs are among the most famous in the short history of photography.

1895–1965

JOAN MIRÓ

A Surrealist painter from Barcelona in Catalonia, Spain, Miró created both abstract works and lively, colorful images of imagined scenes and creatures. His work celebrated Catalan culture.

1893–1983

BARBARA HEPWORTH

British sculptor Hepworth created forms from wood, metal, and stone that looked like they came from nature but were somehow still abstract. Many of the works have curves and smooth surfaces, like shells or body parts.

1903–1975

SALVADOR DALÍ

The scenes painted by Spanish Surrealist Dalí looked like dreams and nightmares. His strange combinations of objects painted in a realistic way can be jarring for the viewer to look at.

1904–1989

PIET MONDRIAN

Dutch painter Mondrian worked in a completely abstract style from the 1910s. He is best known for painting grids of horizontal and vertical lines filled with squares of primary colors.

1872–1944

PAUL KLEE

Known for his abstract, colorful works, Swiss painter Klee wanted his images to look simple, but he worked them out in great detail. Klee's style spread through his teaching position at the Bauhaus, a German art school.

1879–1940

SONIA DELAUNAY

French artist Delaunay was part of the Orphism movement, known for its crisp, geometric forms and bold colors. This style is seen in her paintings and also in her textiles and clothing.

1885–1979

DIEGO RIVERA

Mexican artist Rivera was known for painting large murals (wall paintings). Many of his images showed his strong political beliefs and featured workers or important scenes from history.

1886–1957

FRIDA KAHLO

Mexican artist Kahlo worked in a dreamlike, Surrealist style centered on her own inner world. She painted numerous self-portraits when she was confined to her bed with injuries and illnesses.

1907–1954

JACKSON POLLOCK

The dripped and splattered paintings created by Pollock were highlights of the American movement known as Abstract Expressionism. This style made New York City the center of the modern art world for the first time.

1912–1956

103

WHAT'S THE POINT OF LOOKING AT CONTEMPORARY ART?

From the 1960s, artists broke down many of the barriers that separated painting and sculpture from other forms of art. They took techniques and styles from less "highbrow" sources, such as magazines and comic books. Artworks became unique blends of concepts, sometimes using the artist's body, light, video, sounds, or any number of unusual materials. Contemporary art is often difficult to interpret, as it can be deeply personal to the artist. There are no rules to artistic creativity—artists today can forge new paths or pick and choose ideas from all of art history—and so can you!

HOW TO MAKE YOUR ART POP

In the 1950s and 1960s, a kind of art called Pop Art ("Pop" is short for popular) appeared in Britain and America. Pop artists wanted art to reflect their own young, modern, everyday lives. They rejected accepted ideas about what "good" art should be, and instead turned to popular sources for their images and techniques, such as comics, TV, movies, pop music, shopping, and advertising.

MASS PRODUCTION

Many Pop artists were influenced by mass production, where lots of similar products are made rapidly. So their art often showed ordinary, mass-produced items, repeated similar images, or used mechanical techniques such as printing rather than painting.

Campbell's Soup Cans, 1962, Andy Warhol

Inspiration for Pop Art included the eye-catching colors and designs of modern product packaging.

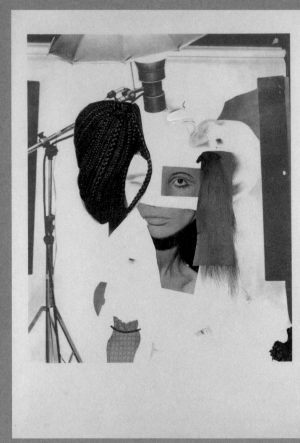

Fashion-Plate (Cosmetic-Study VII),
1969, Richard Hamilton

CUT OUT AND PASTE

Pop artists often used a mix of techniques and sources to create a collage. By using images cut out of magazines, they pointed out that not every aspect of an artwork had to be original.

CELEBRITY

As watching TV became more and more popular, pop stars, actors, and politicians became major celebrities. Pop Art celebrated these famous people because they were a glamorous part of ever-changing modern life.

Colour Her Gone, 1962, Pauline Boty

Hollywood stars were ideal Pop Art subjects.

"HIGH" AND "LOW" ART

Pop artists disagreed with traditional ideas about what was "high" (good and tasteful) and "low" (bad and in poor taste) in art. They thought that artworks with images like those in comics were just as good as oil paintings of landscapes—and more interesting to people of their generation.

Acrylic paint was perfect for Pop Art's bold, hard-edged areas of flat color.

HOW TO PLAY WITH VISION

Op Art ("Op" is short for optical) was a 1960s abstract art movement that used the science behind how we see to stimulate viewers' eyes. It played with optical illusions—when the eye and brain work together to play tricks on you. Op Art contains patterns, geometric shapes, and bold coloring that make images seem to change shape, move, or flicker.

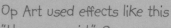

Vega-WA-3, 1968, Victor Vasarely

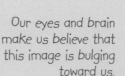

Our eyes and brain make us believe that this image is bulging toward us.

DISTORTION

Op artists cleverly arranged space, shapes, and color so that their images appeared distorted (twisted out of shape). For example, if you paint a circle pattern, but make the circles different sizes and bend their shapes, you can create illusions of depth and movement.

The pyramid shapes can be viewed as pointing outwards.

The pyramid shapes can be viewed as pointing inwards.

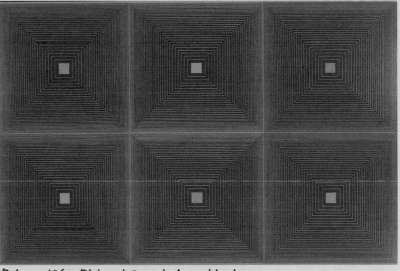

Prisma, 1968, Richard Joseph Anuszkiewicz

AMBIGUITY

Contrasting colors were popular in Op Art because they help produce powerful illusions that may be ambiguous—where viewers can "see" different images within one artwork. Combining contrasting colors is good for creating ambiguous depth effects.

TRY IT OUT
OPTICAL ILLUSION

Make your own piece of Op Art! Using a ruler, start by drawing a square. Inside that, draw smaller, evenly spaced squares, one inside the next. Keep going until you finish with a tiny solid square in the middle.

Artist
BRIDGET RILEY

British Op artist Riley was interested in the sensations and emotions produced by colors and shapes. Carefully placing certain colors next to each other, and using lines or repeated shapes precisely, she created images that look like they are constantly moving and changing, while at the same time feeling calm.

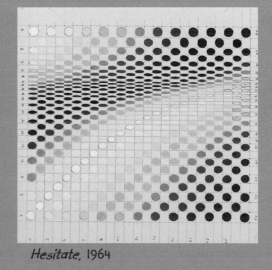

Hesitate, 1964

HOW TO SPREAD A MESSAGE

When people wish to protest for or against issues, promote ideas, or educate people, there is often no need for words. Art and images have been used to communicate messages for centuries. Just one simple, bold graphic on a poster or placard can often be understood by people around the world, no matter what language they speak.

Protest and performance
The international Red Rebel Brigade draw the public's attention to climate problems with performance art. Their red clothes, white-painted faces, and slow movement are consistent across their performances.

Red Rebel Brigade performance, 2023

Earth images clearly suggest climate issues.

BOLD DESIGNS

Strong colors and bold, simple shapes grab attention instantly and forcefully. Many posters created by American artist Keith Haring in the 1980s criticized people who did nothing about the dangerous illness AIDS.

IGNORANCE = FEAR

SILENCE = DEATH

FIGHT AIDS ACT UP

©K.Haring 89

Poster for the ACT UP AIDS awareness campaign, 1989, Keith Haring

This international peace symbol also promotes the Campaign for Nuclear Disarmament.

A rainbow is the perfect symbol for the many identities of the LGBTQ+ community.

CODED COLORS

Many movements use specific colors so people know what their images stand for. In the early 20th century, the British campaign to give women suffrage (full voting rights) used green, purple, and white in their posters and banners.

Poster for *Votes for Women* newspaper, 1910, Hilda Dallas

SYMBOLS

Strong visual symbols give protest movements an identity that people can easily recognize. The raised fist suggests powerful, united resistance. It has been used for various causes, including Black people's rights.

The colors of the women's suffrage movement were purple for dignity, green for hope, and white for purity.

111

HOW TO WORK WITH NATURE

Many artists work with, or in, nature—perhaps to highlight nature's beauty, to comment on people's relationship with nature, or to draw attention to climate change. In the 1960s and 1970s, some artists left their studios and took their work outside. They made art from the landscape itself, such as huge sculptures made from earth and rocks. These artists pioneered the "Land Art" movement.

NATURAL CYCLES

Many artists create works that change depending on nature's cycles, such as the tides of the sea or the position of the Sun. These artworks draw our attention to these cycles, making us think about planet Earth and our place on it.

TEMPORARY ART

Some nature artists like to create works that don't last for long, unlike the paintings and stone sculptures of traditional art. British artist Richard Long made a track by walking back and forth across a field, then photographed it before it vanished.

Land Art often focuses on how humans have an impact on the natural world.

An artwork of stones on a beach will be covered up twice a day when the tide comes in.

A Line Made by Walking, 1967, Richard Long

TRY IT OUT
MAKE LAND ART

You can make amazing patterns, shapes, and structures from anything natural, such as leaves, twigs, fir cones, and stones. Remember: never damage or uproot nature, take away things that others could enjoy, or remove pebbles from a beach.

Land Art might be experienced differently depending on the time of day or the weather.

Artworks grown from seeds can take many years to mature into their final form.

Artist
OLAFUR ELIASSON

Icelandic Danish installation artist Eliasson produces striking, nature-based artworks that are often designed to surprise or involve viewers. He has placed large blocks of melting ice outside galleries to draw attention to global warming and created the illusion of a massive indoor sun. For *Fog assembly*, he created a constant mist that looked different depending on the changing sun and wind conditions.

ART THAT GROWS

The passage of time is often a feature of Land Art. Sonfist's *The Monument of the Lost Falcon*, which will grow and change over time, highlighting the disappearance of the falcon from its natural habitat.

The Monument of the Lost Falcon, photographed in 2014, Alan Sonfist

Fog assembly, 2016

HOW TO MAKE A SCENE

Around the 1960s, artists began to question the idea that an artwork must be a separate, permanent, single piece of art. This led to the appearance of the first installations—scenes created from various pieces of art. Artists make installations to work in a particular space, where viewers can move around them and become part of them. Installations can be indoors or outdoors, permanent or temporary.

Video can add elements such as voice and movement.

SCULPTURE

Installation artists have pioneered sculptures in nontraditional materials, even inflatables. Often, a sculpture counts as an installation because it takes over the space and involves viewers.

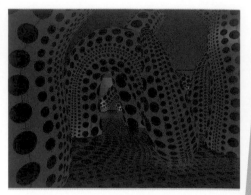

A Bouquet of Love I Saw in the Universe, 2021, Yayoi Kusama

Putting an artwork on the floor makes the viewer move around it.

ART CONNECTIONS

Performance art
Artworks can take the form of an event that is performed in front of a live audience. The artist is frequently the performer. Performance art is often linked with installation art—interaction is a major part of both of them.

The Artist Is Present, 2010, Marina Abramović, in which the artist stared at visitors who took turns sitting opposite her.

LIGHT AND SOUND

To create the feeling that an artwork surrounds the viewer, artists might use light and sound. American artist Dan Flavin developed light installations, and Japanese artist Yuri Suzuki explores sound. Both help to connect the viewer more closely to the art.

The Welcome Chorus,
2019/2020, Yuri Suzuki

SPACE

Some installations use space by creating obstacles that block the viewer from easily moving around them. Others create paths the viewer can use to navigate their way through the installation.

Naming the Money,
2004, Lubaina Himid

DID YOU KNOW?

The Berlin Wall

A wall that once split the city of Berlin, Germany, into two came down in 1989. A section of the wall was decorated with street-style art to mark this event.

Alles Offen (Everything's Open), 1990, Rosemarie Schinzler

BANKSY

Making street art without permission is usually illegal, so some artists work in secret. "Banksy," who chooses to hide his identity, uses stencils to produce his illegal art quickly.

HOW TO TAKE IT TO THE STREET

From the 1970s, writing, drawing, or painting on public walls and buildings developed into a bold, rebellious, and expressive art form. Young people wanted to make their voices heard in their own way. Street art and graffiti styles were influenced by images made for political street protests in the late 1960s and by the speed and ease of painting with spray cans.

A paint roller creates large, blocky shapes quickly.

Pedro Luján and His Dog, 2012, Martín Ron

Mural in Dakar, Senegal, by Docta and others

MARTÍN RON

Detailed murals (wall paintings) often look like the kinds of paintings you might see in a gallery. Work by Argentinian artist Martín Ron combines realism, fantasy, and huge size to create an impact.

DOCTA

Much street art focuses on bringing political and social issues into public view. Senegalese artist Docta has participated in street art awareness campaigns about racism, AIDS, malaria, and COVID-19.

Stenciling involves spraying paint over a shape cut out of paper or card stock.

Rapid freehand work with a spray can is skillful and creates a spontaneous feel.

Street artists often cover their faces with masks to avoid inhaling aerosol and paint fumes.

WHAT IS ART?

Street art and graffiti

The difference between street art and graffiti isn't always clear. The term "street art" is often used to describe legal art that is image-based, while "graffiti" often refers to illegal, text-based art. But there isn't a clear distinction, so how do we tell them apart?

HOW TO MAKE IT PUBLIC

Ever since the 1950s, art—especially sculpture—has moved from galleries and formal spaces to places where people live and work. Many believe art improves our surroundings and has a positive impact on our mental health, so it should be available to everyone. Compared to older traditions, modern public art can appear in unexpected places. It might be made from unusual materials, or depict less traditional subjects.

PLACES

Public sculptures were once displayed mostly in spaces where lots of people gathered, such as town squares. Today, they are found on rooftops, at the side of highways, on beaches, and even under water.

Many traditional sculptures were placed high up on a plinth (platform) to make them more impressive.

Angel of the North, 1998, Antony Gormley, Gateshead, Tyne and Wear, England

MATERIALS

Durable substances, such as stone and bronze, were popular traditional choices for outdoor sculptures. Modern artists like to experiment with varied materials, from polished steel that reflects a sculpture's surroundings to recycled street rubbish and living plants.

Polished white marble—a kind of stone—was a favorite material of sculptors until the 20th century.

La Nouvelle Liberté (The New Statue of Liberty), 1996, Joseph-Francis Sumégné, Deïdo, Douala, Cameroon

SUBJECTS

Public sculptures used to depict important people or historic events. Today, a sculpture's subject may not be obvious. It might express something meaningful to the artist or hold no deep meaning at all. This can make it hard to understand—especially if the style is abstract.

Traditional Western sculpture used styles that made subjects easily recognizable

Floralis Genérica, 2002, Eduardo Catalano, Plaza de las Naciones Unidas, Buenos Aires, Argentina

Artist
LOUISE BOURGEOIS

Modern sculpture is often autobiographical—inspired by the artist's own life. French American artist Bourgeois came from a family of tapestry weavers. Spiders, known for weaving complex webs, were an important subject in her art, and a tribute to her weaver mother.

Maman (Mum/Mom), 1999, Guggenheim Museum, Bilbao, Basque Country, Spain

119

Duvor Cloth, 2007, El Anatsui

EL ANATSUI

A sculptor from Ghana, Anatsui creates metal sculptures that look like hanging textiles, using objects found in local recycling stations. His method for pounding the metal into shape resembles techniques used to beat gold mined in West Africa during colonial times.

HOW TO CELEBRATE YOUR HERITAGE

Western artists have been inspired by the artistic traditions of other cultures for many centuries. But non-Western art has often been sidelined or undervalued by the Western art establishment. It is only recently that art and artists from non-Western cultures have become more well known and respected in the West. Today, non-Western artists shine a light on the artistic traditions of their own cultures and combine them with Western art to create something new and entirely their own.

Pintura Peruana (Peruvian Painting),
2021, Andrés Argüelles Vigo

Space Walk, 2002, Yinka Shonibare

ANDRÉS ARGÜELLES VIGO

Peruvian artist Vigo looks at the relationship between art and history. He recreates old portraits of Peruvian leaders but adapts them, taking out or blurring elements, or adding modern objects such as drink cans. His works also highlight how Indigenous Andean peoples have been ignored in Peruvian art.

YINKA SHONIBARE

The best-known sculptures of British Nigerian artist Shonibare are his figures clothed in colorful African Batik fabric. By using this material on figures who the viewer would not expect to be African, he explores issues of race and identity.

DID YOU KNOW?

Art and colonialism
Many non-Western artists produce works that deal with the colonial history of their countries, when European powers took control and exploited the native peoples. Combining the two artistic traditions of colonizer and colonized allows artists to examine how colonialism has affected their country.

121

HOW TO USE THE LATEST TECH

Art has always changed with the times, but since the late 20th century, the advancement of computers and digital technology has brought with it many new ways to create and appreciate art. Some artists now create their work digitally, allowing them to make exciting art that doesn't have to be an object in the physical world. Even technology itself has got in on the act—with human assistance, artist robots and powerful artificial intelligence (AI) programs are able to create their own art.

A variety of accessories are available to digital artists, including the touchscreen pen (known as a stylus).

Digital art applications offer lots of tools that allow artists to manipulate their work.

DIGITAL TOOLS

Software for creating art on a computer, tablet, or other digital device can mimic artistic effects such as brushstrokes made from paint. Art made digitally can also incorporate things traditional art cannot, such as animation.

Self-portrait by Ai-Da, first exhibited in 2021

Ai-Da can speak, form facial expressions, and track people's faces, making her appear to react to her surroundings.

WHAT IS ART?

AI-generated art

The development of AI art has happened so quickly that many of the issues surrounding the topic are still under discussion. Some people believe that art is a uniquely human activity and that machines will never create art without some form of human creative input. Can you see a future filled with machine artists?

Ai-Da's robotic arm allows her to hold a pencil or paintbrush and to paint using a palette.

AI-DA

The world's first humanoid robot artist, Ai-Da is able to paint using her robotic arm, the cameras in her eyes, and her AI programming. Her work has been shown in major galleries, and, as she is equipped for speech, she has given talks about the future of art at various institutions.

Artist
NAM JUNE PAIK

In the 1960s, when television was first becoming popular, Korean American artist Paik created a whole new type of art known as video art. He made sculptures and installations that included screens playing video and often sound. He also became well known for his robots made of TV and radio parts.

TV is Kitsch, 1996

123

CONTEMPORARY ARTISTS

Artworks created by contemporary artists are full of variety—there are no rules. The subjects they cover range from powerful emotions to political messages to works of abstract beauty. Some artists use their own bodies in works of performance art, while others create sculptures from everyday materials such as recycled items.

EMILY KAME KNGWARREYE

First Nation Australian artist Kngwarreye started painting in her late 70s. Her colorful, abstract works represent Dreaming sites, important places in Aboriginal culture.

1910–1996

DORIS SALCEDO

The troubled history of Salcedo's native Colombia is a great influence on her work, which examines how war and violence affect people's lives. Ordinary household items form the basis of much of her art.

MARINA ABRAMOVIĆ

One of the most famous performance artists in the world, Abramović uses her own body in interactive performances. She explores themes such as trust and survival in her work.

1946–

1958–

JEAN-MICHEL BASQUIAT

Associated with graffiti and street art, Basquiat's raw, unfinished-looking works had bold colors and often resembled simple childhood drawings. His art tackled important topics, such as racism.

TAKASHI MURAKAMI

With the brightly colored cartoons and flowers that often appear in his works, Japanese Pop artist Murakami blurs the boundary between popular culture and fine art.

1960–1988

1962–

ANDY WARHOL

In the 1960s, Warhol became famous for his repeated imagery of everyday items, such as soup cans and Coca-Cola bottles. In his view, art is all around us—at the grocery store, the movie theater, or in a magazine.

YAYOI KUSAMA

Japanese artist Kusama is known for her "infinity rooms" full of mirrors and lights. She uses repetition of abstract forms, most famously polka dots.

1928-1987

1929-

FAITH RINGGOLD

An important icon for Black, feminist, American art, Ringgold's paintings and quilts often contain messages encouraging social change.

EL ANATSUI

Ghanaian sculptor Anatsui uses found objects such as bottle caps and tin cans in his work. When sewn together, they look like luxurious woven tapestries.

1930-

1944-

YINKA SHONIBARE

British Nigerian artist Shonibare is known for his sculptures of figures dressed in vividly colored African Batik fabric. The international origins of this material reflect Shonibare's interest in the complex topic of nationality.

TRACEY EMIN

British artist Emin rose to prominence in the 1990s with her personal and revealing works. She uses a variety of art forms, including sculptures and installations.

1962-

1963-

GLOSSARY

ABSTRACT ART

An artistic style founded in the early 20th century that uses shapes and colors to represent subjects or emotions, instead of depicting people, objects, and scenes in a recognizable way.

ABSTRACT EXPRESSIONISM

This movement began in the 1940s in New York. Art was typically created with strong brushstrokes and industrial paints.

ACRYLIC PAINT

A plastic-based paint that dries quickly.

ACTION PAINTING

An artistic technique where the process of painting is as important as the finished work.

APPRENTICE

A young person sent to help and learn from an artist.

ART MOVEMENT

A period of time when a group of artists produce work with similar themes or techniques.

ART NOUVEAU

A decorative, floral style popular between the 1890s and early 20th century.

AUTOMATISM

The technique of creating art in a random way, led by the unconscious mind. This method is often used in Surrealist works.

BAROQUE

A style of art and architecture popular in 17th-century Europe and Latin America. It is grand and theatrical.

CALLIGRAPHY

Decorative or ornamental writing. In East Asia and the Islamic world, in particular, artists use brushes and ink to transform script into works of art.

CANVAS

A material made from sturdy cloth that artists can paint on.

CHIAROSCURO

A strong, dramatic contrast between light and shade in a painting.

CLASSICAL

Describes ancient Greek or Roman art, especially sculpture.

COLLAGE

An image that is made of a variety of materials stuck on to a flat surface.

COMPOSITION

How the artist decides to place things or people in an artwork.

CONCEPTUAL ART

An artistic style where the idea or meaning behind a piece of art is more important than what it looks like.

CUBISM

Emerging in early 20th-century Europe, this style of painting shows objects or people from different viewpoints at the same time, breaking them up into odd angles and fragments.

DADA

An art movement that led to strange and shocking works of art, born out of the horrors of World War I.

DE STIJL

This Dutch movement, which encompasses Neoplasticism, emphasized harmonious forms and primary colors.

DUTCH GOLDEN AGE

A period spanning most of the 17th century, where the Netherlands was the leading European power in the arts, trade, and science.

EN PLEIN AIR

The French expression for painting "in open air," referring to the style of many 19th-century Impressionists who preferred the natural light of the outdoors.

EXHIBITION

A display of several artworks by one or many artists. Exhibitions are usually held in galleries.

EXPOSURE

In photography, the amount of light that enters the camera lens to take a photograph.

EXPRESSIONISM

This art movement emerged in the 20th century and emphasized distorted or exaggerated objects, people, and colors to express the inner lives and emotions of the artists.

FAUVISM

This early 20th-century movement was typified by artists' use of simplified shapes, bold brushstrokes, and vibrant color to express a sense of wild, energetic emotion.

FIGURATIVE ART

An artistic style that depicts people, scenes, and objects in a recognizable way.

FORESHORTENING

In painting, a term for making an object or person seem to project forward, toward the observer.

FRESCO

A technique of painting, usually on a wall, using a mixture of powdered pigments and water on wet plaster.

GEOMETRIC

Made from recognizable shapes, such as squares and triangles, or bold lines.

GOTHIC

A western European style of art and architecture that flourished in western Europe between the 12th and 15th centuries.

GRAFFITI

An image or inscription on a wall, often made without permission.

HIEROGLYPHS

An ancient Egyptian writing system that used symbols and pictures to convey meaning.

ICON

In painting, this term refers to an image that depicts Jesus Christ, the Virgin Mary, a saint, or another holy person.

ILLUMINATED MANUSCRIPT

A handwritten book, usually from the Middle Ages, that is filled with intricate images and decorated letters.

IMPRESSIONISM

An artistic movement beginning in France in the 1860s. Its painters wanted to create an "impression" of their subjects, recreating effects of light and color with rapid brushstrokes.

INSTALLATION

Three-dimensional artwork that is set up, or installed, in a space.

LAND ART

An art style where artists use natural materials and often site their work in a natural setting.

LANDSCAPE

1. A painting or photograph of natural scenery, like mountains, rivers, or farmland.
2. A format of painting or photograph that is wider than it is tall.

MEDIEVAL

A term that is used to describe European art from the Middle Ages (the period in Europe between the 5th and mid-15th centuries).

MODERN ART

Some art that was made from the late 19th century to the late 20th century, by artists who tried out various new ideas and methods.

MODERNISM

A broad term for describing beliefs, attitudes, art, and architecture from the beginning of the 20th century.

MOSAIC

The technique of producing images by combining small pieces of glass, stone, pottery, or other hard materials.

MURAL

A big painting made on a wall.

NEOCLASSICISM

A style that was inspired by ancient Greek and Roman art and architecture. It became popular in the late 18th and early 19th centuries.

NEOPLASTICISM

An abstract style of painting, using only rectangles, straight lines, and a small number of colors.

OIL PAINT

A type of paint that dries very slowly and is made by mixing pigments of color with oil, such as flaxseed.

OP ART

A form of abstract art that uses certain colors and patterns to make images look as if they are changing shape, moving, or flickering.

PERFORMANCE ART

An art style where artists create their work through actions. The artist is often the performer.

PERSPECTIVE

The technique used to depict something three-dimensional, such as a building or person, on a flat surface.

POINTILLISM

A painting technique that consists of tiny dots of different colors placed close together. Seen from a distance, these dots combine into a complete picture.

POP ART

An artistic style from the 1950s and 1960s that is based on popular culture, especially using images from comic books and advertisements.

PORTRAIT

1. A painting or photograph of a person or group of people. A self-portrait is a painting or photograph of the artist by him- or herself.
2. Describes an image format that is taller than it is wide.

POSTIMPRESSIONISM

A catch-all term encompassing different types of art movements and artistic techniques that followed Impressionism.

PRIMITIVE ART

A term to describe tribal and folk art from around the world.

PRINTMAKING

A method of making many copies of one image.

REALISM

An art movement that began in the 1850s, showing life, people, and everyday subjects in a realistic way.

RENAISSANCE

A movement inspired by the artistic ideals of ancient Greece and Rome, which began in Italy in the 14th century and then spread to other parts of Europe. Also refers to the historic period between the 14th and 16th centuries.

ROCOCO

A light, playful art style popular in 18th-century Europe, often featuring idyllic scenes.

ROMANTICISM

A 19th-century movement in which artists painted in a dramatic, emotional style, often showing a person surrounded by a wild or stormy landscape.

SCULPTURE

Art created by carving, shaping, or molding materials such as marble, clay, or wood into abstract or realistic figures.

SFUMATO

A method of gradually blending colors in a painting to create blurred, soft outlines.

STILL LIFE

A painting of objects such as fruit or flowers, arranged decoratively.

SUBJECT

Something that an artist has decided to paint or photograph.

SUPREMATISM

One of the earliest forms of abstract art, created by the Russian artist Kazimir Malevich from 1913. He painted groups of circles, squares, triangles, and other geometric forms.

SURREALISM

An art style beginning in the 1920s that aimed to illustrate dreams and the unconscious mind, often showing objects in odd combinations or confusing sceneries.

SYMBOLISM

A poetic, mysterious art style appearing in the late 19th century as a reaction to Realism and Impressionism.

WESTERN ART

The art of the European countries, and those countries that share cultural traditions with Europe—such as the nations of North America.

WOODBLOCK PRINTING

The Asian method of carving an image into a block of wood, covering the uncarved surfaces with ink, and pressing it onto paper.

INDEX

ACKNOWLEDGMENTS

DK would like to thank the following people for their assistance in the preparation of this book:

Assistant Picture Research Administrator: Manpreet Kaur; editorial assistance: Edward Aves; proofreading: Victoria Pyke; index: Elizabeth Wise.

The publisher would like to thank the following for their kind permission to reproduce their photographs:

(Key: a-above; b-below/bottom; c-center; f-far; l-left; r-right; t-top)

11 Alamy Stock Photo: agefotostock / J.D. Dallet (br). 12 Alamy Stock Photo: Historic Images (cra). Dreamstime.com: Sergio Bertino (br). 13 Alamy Stock Photo: GRANGER - Historical Picture Archive (tr). Parks Australia: (bc). 14 Alamy Stock Photo: CPA Media Pte Ltd / Pictures From History (c). 16 Dreamstime.com: Michal Janoek / Wesleycl701 (cra). 17 Alamy Stock Photo: Michael DeFreitas Asia (cra); Mark Phillips (bl). 18 Alamy Stock Photo: History & Art Collection (cl). 19 Dreamstime.com: Geografika (cr); Erick Nguyen / Erickn (crb). 20 Alamy Stock Photo: funkyfood London - Paul Williams (bc). 21 Alamy Stock Photo: Penta Springs Limited / Artokoloro (bl). 22 Alamy Stock Photo: Lanmas (bc). 23 Bridgeman Images: (cra). 27 Alamy Stock Photo: Crystite RF (cb); IanDagnall Computing (tl); Tjetjep Rustandi (tc); Nancy Carter / North Wind Picture Archives (tr). 28 Bridgeman Images: (br). 30 Alamy Stock Photo: SuperStock / David David Gallery (cra). 31 Alamy Stock Photo: Mariano Garcia (ca); Graham Prentice (tr). Bridgeman Images: Photo © Christie's Images (bl). 32 Alamy Stock Photo: CPA Media Pte Ltd / Pictures From History (cra); Penta Springs Limited / Artokoloro (bc). 33 Alamy Stock Photo: DIT Archive (tl); robertharding / Christian Kober (br); ErnestoGravelpond / © Banco de México Diego Rivera Frida Kahlo Museums Trust, Mexico, D.F. / DACS 2023. (bl). 34 Alamy Stock Photo: ART Collection 4 (tr). 35 Bridgeman Images: (cra). 37 Dorling Kindersley: Gary Ombler / Durham University Oriental Museum (tc). 38 Dreamstime.com: Ankal2 (br). 42 Alamy Stock Photo: INTERFOTO / Personalities (c). 44 Alamy Stock Photo: ART Collection (cra). 45 Alamy Stock Photo: IanDagnall Computing (br). 46 Bridgeman Images: (br). 47 Bridgeman Images: (tl); © Minneapolis Institute of Art / Bequest of Herschel V. Jones (bc); Photo © Raffaello Bencini (br). 48 Alamy Stock Photo: Eyal Bartov (br). 49 Dorling Kindersley: CONACULTA-INAH-MEX / Michel Zabé (crb). 54 Alamy Stock Photo: World History Archive (cra). 55 Alamy Stock Photo: Peter Horree (tc); Peter Loud (br). Bridgeman Images: Museum of Fine Arts, Houston / Museum purchase funded by Robert J. Cruikshank in honor of Mr. and Mrs.

Meredith Long at "One Great Night in November" (tr); Photo © Bonhams, London, UK (tl). 56 Alamy Stock Photo: agefotostock / Historical Views (br). The Metropolitan Museum of Art: H. O. Havemeyer Collection, Bequest of Mrs. H. O. Havemeyer, 1929 (cb). 57 Brooklyn Museum: Gift of Anna Ferris (br). 58 Alamy Stock Photo: Nikreates (cra). 59 Alamy Stock Photo: ART Collection (br); FineArt (cf). 60 Alamy Stock Photo: Pictures Now (tr). Rijksmuseum, Amsterdam: On loan from the City of Amsterdam (br). 63 Bridgeman Images: Wallace Collection, London, UK (br). 64 Alamy Stock Photo: Penta Springs Limited / Gibon Art (br). Bridgeman Images: Reproduced by permission of Chatsworth Settlement Trustees (br). 65 Alamy Stock Photo: Josse Christophel (br). 70 Bridgeman Images: Luisa Ricciarini (br). 71 Alamy Stock Photo: Uber Bilder (br). Bridgeman Images: (tc). 72 Alamy Stock Photo: © Fine Art Images / Heritage Images (br). 73 Alamy Stock Photo: Hi-Story (cr). Bridgeman Images: Luisa Ricciarini (cf). 74 Alamy Stock Photo: Thunderstruck (bl). 75 The University of Arizona Museum of Art & Archive of Visual Arts, Tucson: Collection Center for Creative Photography, University of Arizona. © The Ansel Adams Publishing Rights Trust / Photograph by Ansel Adams (br). 76 Alamy Stock Photo: agefotostock / Historical Views (cra); World History Archive (cra). 77 Alamy Stock Photo: Penta Springs Limited / Artokoloro (bl); World History Archive (cra). 78 Bridgeman Images: Helen Birch Bartlett Memorial Collection (bl). 79 Alamy Stock Photo: C8W (bl). Bridgeman Images: (br). 80 Alamy Stock Photo: Bill Waterson (cr). 81 Alamy Stock Photo: Album (bl); Bildarchiv Monheim GmbH / Florian Monheim (cra). 82 Alamy Stock Photo: Giorgio Morara (bc). The Metropolitan Museum of Art: Harris Brisbane Dick Fund, 1932 (crb). 83 Alamy Stock Photo: © Fine Art Images / Heritage Images (tc); Lebrecht Music & Arts (clb). Bridgeman Images: (cr). 88 Bridgeman Images: Luisa Ricciarini (c). 89 Bridgeman Images: © National Museums Scotland (tl); © Succession H. Matisse/ DACS 2023 (crb). 90 Getty Images / iStock: LUKel138 (bc). 91 Bridgeman Images: National Gallery of Victoria, Melbourne / © Succession Picasso/DACS, London 2023 (br); The Phillips Collection, Washington, D.C., USA / Acquired 1934 / © ADAGP, Paris and DACS, London 2023 (tc). 92 Philadelphia Museum of Art: The Louise and Walter Arensberg Collection, 1950 (br). 93 Photo Scala, Florence: Digital image, The Museum of Modern Art, New York / © Association Marcel Duchamp / ADAGP, Paris and DACS, London 2023. (br). 94 Alamy Stock Photo: Artefact (cf); Peter Barritt (br). 95 Alamy Stock Photo: Mariano Garcia (tl); © Fine Art Images / Heritage Images (cr); Iain Masterton (bc). 96 Alamy Stock Photo: Salvador Dali, Fundació Gala-Salvador Dalí, DACS 2023. (cb). Getty Images: RDB / ullstein bild / © DACS 2023 (c). 97 Bridgeman Images: Photo © Christie's Images / © ADAGP, Paris and DACS, London 2023. (br). 98 Bridgeman Images: © Art Institute of Chicago / Friends of American Art Collection (bc). 99 Bridgeman Images: Art Institute of Chicago / Gift of Leigh B. Block / © Georgia O'Keeffe Museum / DACS 2023. (br). 100 Alamy Stock Photo: Edward Westmacott / © The Pollock-Krasner Foundation ARS, NY and DACS, London 2023 (br). 101 ©

Helen Frankenthaler Foundation, Inc. / ARS, NY and DACS, London 2023 (br). 106 Bridgeman Images: © 2023 The Andy Warhol Foundation for the Visual Arts, Inc. / Licensed by DACS, London / SuperStock (clb); Photo © Christie's Images / © R. Hamilton. All Rights Reserved, DACS 2023. (cr). 107 Bridgeman Images: © Wolverhampton Art Gallery / Courtesy of the Pauline Boty Estate/Whitford Fine Art (cla). 108 Bridgeman Images: © Davis Museum at Wellesley College / Bequest of Dr. Ruth Boschwitz Benedict (Class of 1935) / © ADAGP, Paris and DACS, London 2023. (cf). 109 Bridgeman Images: © Cleveland Museum of Art / Gift of Katherine C. White / © The estate of Richard Anuszkiewicz/VAGA at ARS, NY and DACS, London 2023 (br); Photo Scala, Florence: Christie's Images, London / Copyright Bridget Riley 2023. All rights reserved (br). 110 Alamy Stock Photo: Orlando Britain (cra). Keith Haring artwork © Keith Haring Foundation: (clb). 111 Alamy Stock Photo: incamerastock / ICP (ca). 112 © DACS / Artimage 2023: Richard Long. All Rights Reserved, DACS/Artimage 2023. Photo: Richard Long (clb). 113 Alamy Stock Photo: Hans Blossey (bl); Courtesy of the artist; neugerriemschneider, Berlin; Tanya Bonakdar Gallery, New York / Los Angeles: Photo: Anders Sune Berg © 2016 Olafur Eliasson (br). 114 Alamy Stock Photo: Associated Press / Mary Altaffer (cb); Yula Zubritsky / Art by YAYOI KUSAMA (cra). 115 Alamy Stock Photo: Trevor Chriss. Pentagram Design / Yuri Suzuki (t); Installation view, 'Navigation Charts, 2017 © Spike Island, Bristol Photo: Stuart Whipps. Courtesy the artist, Hollybush Gardens, and National Museums, Liverpool. (bl). 116 Alamy Stock Photo: imageBROKER.com GmbH & Co. KG / Wilfried Wirth (cla); Dmytro Surkov (tr). 117 Alamy Stock Photo: agefotostock / Christian Goupi. Docta- Doxandem Squad (tr); Associated Press / Natacha Pisarenko / Permission by Martin Ron (tl). 118 Alamy Stock Photo: PA Images / Owen Humphreys (tl). 119 Alamy Stock Photo: Diego Grandi (cr); Peter Treanor (tr); Sérgio Nogueira / © The Easton Foundation/VAGA at ARS, NY and DACS, London 2023. (br). 120 Bridgeman Images: © Indianapolis Museum of Art / Ann M. Stack Fund for Contemporary Art (tr). 121 Andrés Argüelles Vigo: "Pintura Peruana" Oil con canvas 110 x 120 cm 2021 (tl); The Fabric Workshop and Museum (FWM): Yinka Shonibare CBE RA, in collaboration with The Fabric Workshop and Museum, Philadelphia. Space Walk, 2002. Fiberglass, silkscreen print on cotton sateen and cotton brocade, and plastic. Dimensions vary with installation. Edition 1 of 2 / Aaron Igler; All Rights Reserved. © DACS 2023. (tr). 123 Alamy Stock Photo: PA Images / David Parry / Ai-Da ROBOT (tl). Bridgeman Images: Photo © Christie's Images / TV is Kitsch, 1996 (mixed media) / © Nam June Paik Estate (br)

All other images © Dorling Kindersley

WHAT WILL YOU DISCOVER NEXT?

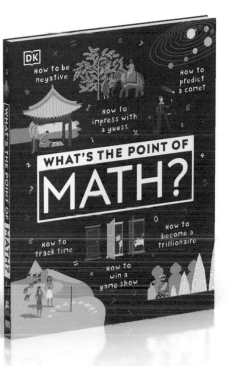

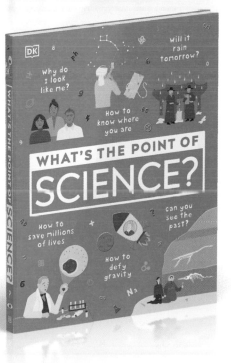